Child Labour

Theory, Conventions and Experiences

To

Bhaijaan

Prof. M.Y.M. Siddiqui

Who shaped my career

Child Labour

Theory, Conventions and Experiences

M.I. Siddiqui
Department of Applied & Regional Economics
M.J.P. Rohilkhand University, Bareilly

ANAMIKA PUBLISHERS & DISTRIBUTORS (P) LTD.
4697/3, 21-A, Ansari Road, Daryaganj
New Delhi-110 002
Phone : 23281655

First Published, 2005

ISBN 81-7975-026-4

PRINTED IN INDIA

Published by Anamika Publishers & Distributors (P) Ltd., 4697/3, 21-A, Ansari Road, Daryaganj, New Delhi-110 002. Typeset by Nidhi Laser Point, Shahdara Delhi and Printed at Nagri Printers, Delhi.

CONTENTS

ACKNOWLEDGEMENT

The author gratefully acknowledges discussions with **Mr. V. Subrahmaniya, IMF Advisor** to the National Bank of Eritrea and former Executive Director of the R.B.I. He aroused my interest in the theoretical aspects of child labour.

Mr. Yash Kapur at the **United Nations Headquarter**, New York has not only encouraged but also gave certain important tips regarding the work on working children based on his vast experience.

Some of the experiences shared by **Mr. Khalid Siddiqui** of the UNHCR shed light especially on displaced children due to war and other calamities who ultimately drift into labour market.

Dr. Vishwanathan, Deputy General Manager, **NABARD** is acknowledged for his valuable suggestions and experience sharing with the author.

The most arduous task of Proof reading and providing some of the material by my colleague **Israr Khan** is thankfully acknowledged.

Manoj Pandey did computer and graphic work and without his expertise it was not possible to complete the book in time.

My family members **Abha, Samir** and **Amber** deserve special mention and their support is acknowledged lovingly and affectionately.

Thanks are also due to my publisher for timely publication of the book.

PREFACE

Child labour has aroused passion at individual, organizational and, governmental levels. Its elimination has been high on the agenda of every developing country where it is harboured the most. India happens to be the abode of largest number of child workers in the world.

However opinion and perception about child labour differ widely. Even the very concept of child has been in controversy and consequently a number of definitions exist. Similarly perception of child also varies from region to region.

The present book is an attempt to synthesize the *theory-conventions- practices* and hence its subject matter is somewhat different from others. It begins with the theory and then proceeds to elaborate child labour and its variants.

Chapter 2 explains the dynamics of child labour highlighting the role of informal sector responsible for creating space for child labour. Moreover, modes of production giving rise to informal sector have also been discussed in the context of child labour.

The *niches* are taken up in Chapter 3 which infact provides details of important economic activities harbouring child labour. These are agriculture including commercial farming, industry and construction, services and, domestic or household sector. The invisibility factor makes domestic services a strong case to study child labour.

Chapter 4 discusses child labour in the export industries where *sub-contracting* has created ample space for children. Since export falls in the formal sector it is believed that it has no child labour. This formal sector invites more attention of those concerned with child labour where it is supposed to be not existing.

Some regions deserve more attention to combat the problem of child labour since less efforts have been made there. Therefore, dark continent, that is, Africa should be given more emphasis by the international organizations such as ILO and UNICEF. Chapter 5 covers this aspect.

Child labour is associated with hazards which have been enunciated in Chapter 6. It attempts at listing main hazards with respect to child labour. A list of occupations and industries and related hazards have also been discussed. Countries and child labour hazards are also enumerated in this chapter.

Conventions, Laws and Child Rights form one whole chapter. It provides all the necessary details in regard to child labour.

Lastly methodology to study child labour has been given in Chapter 8. Though study on a particular aspect of child labour depends on its own merits, some methodological issues and steps form the core of this chapter.

The book is neither a case study nor a manual for field workers. It basically covers theoretical aspects of child labour, conventions and child rights and hence is a step towards synthesis. If the present work leads to further theorization of child labour it would be an ample reward to the efforts made here. Hope that the book would be taken well by those concerned with the issue.

M.I. Siddiqui

1. INTRODUCTION

THE THEORY-CONVENTION-PRACTICE SYNTHESIS

Child Labour, be it wage-employment, contractual, apprentice or forced and bonded, is employed *per se* for the cost-minimization everywhere. Cheaper the labour, larger the demand for working children. Hence it may be summed-up as

$$D_{Lc} = f(W_{Lc})$$

where D_{Lc} *and* W_{Lc} represent demand for child labour and wage-rate. It is not difficult to surmise inverse relationship in such equations.

Why is it that child labour is cheaper than the adult labour? There is not single factor responsible for it. For one, child labour has a plentiful supply. So, is true for the adult labour. This is second factor which distinguishes child labour from adult labour, that is, illegality of child labour which in turn deprives it from the protection rights such as unionism, minimum wages etc. Child labour has been declared illegal and its elimination has been set an important goal by all the governments irrespective of their state of development. Consequently, in those sectors where regulations are almost non-existent, e.g., agriculture and allied activities, or where meagre, e.g. informal sector and also under the umbrella of family-labour in cottage industry, supply of child labour is 'plentiful' vis-à-vis its demand. Hence lower wage-rate. Therefore

$$W_{Lc} = f(S_{Lc}),$$

wage-rate for child labour depends upon the supply of child labour. This relationship holds good in the absence of implementation of child labour laws and what economists write as 'other things being equal' or more sophistically *ceteris paribus.*

Circular reasoning leads to another question; why does the supply of child labour is abundant or plentiful in developing countries where the problem of child labour persists predominantly? Again the answer is quite handy, i.e., due to high birth rate and out-migration from the rural areas. In the form of notations, it may be expressed as:

$$S_{Lc} = f(b_r, E_0)$$

Where S_{Lc} stands for the supply of child labour, b_r for birth rate and E_0 for emigration from rural to urban centres. Out of these factors, high birth rate is a well-known and rather 'beaten out' factor in the sense that it has been played so much that every one seems to have mugged up. Out-migration, primarily lead us to the informal sector where employment opportunities are a 'pull-factor'. So,

$$E_0 = f(N)$$

Where E_0 and N stand for out-emigration and employment respectively, stating that emigration from rural to urban centres is mainly due to employment possibilities existing in the non-organized sector, lovingly known as informal sector. In this manner, trajection is complete and trajectory may be: *child labour ⇒ Wage-rate ⇒ plentiful supply of working children ⇒ high birth and out migration rates ⇒ child labour* employment in unorganized sector. The system, therefore, be closed as

$$D_{Lc} = f(W_{Lc}) \quad \ldots \quad (1)$$

$$W_{Lc} = f(S_{Lc}) \quad \ldots \quad (2)$$

$$S_{Lc} = f(B_r, E_0) \quad \ldots \quad (3)$$

$$E_0 = f(N) \quad \ldots \quad (4)$$

Where N also includes child labour or demand for child labour, i.e. D_{Lc}. Some manipulations are required to make it possible to solve. Birth rate if taken as given and dropped from equation (3), then the equation is reduced to

$$S_{Lc} = f(E_0) \quad \ldots \quad (3)$$

Still number of equations and unknowns is lopsided, former being four and the later five. Hence an identify may be introduced to balance, i.e.

$$N = D_{Lc}$$

that is employment of child labour is equal to demand for child labour.This identity is $N=D_{Lc}$, is on the presumption that plentiful supply of child labour makes it possible to employ all the child labour which is demanded on the going wage-rate. Now, the system may, theoretically, be solved since number of unknowns equals the number of equations.

Informal and agricultural sectors due to their 'unregulated' nature in developing countries have became harbours of child labour. The former due to its characteristics and latter in the name of family labour. These have also drawn the attention of the international organizations especially with regard to child labour and its employment laced with exploitation. The United Nations in its Declaration in 1959 and later Convention on the Rights of the Child in 1989 have given rise to legislations in various countries, particularly in the Third World (the term seems obscure after the disintegration of socialist nations). The crux of the problem, however, is that the theory of child labour including all its 'push' and 'pull' factors, and conventions implying legislations are not inter-linked to find a solution.

In practice, child labour is a growing problems in all developing countries. How to reconcile theory with conventions and legislations since the former provides space for child labour on various grounds while the latter is bent upon its elimination. The element of 'intervention' – government and non-government both, provides a ray of hope for reconciliation between theory on the one hand, and convention cum practice on the other.

Interventions from the side of the government are generally in the form of strategies, programmes and policies. But government interventions without commitment due to lack of political will, have yielded no significant results so far. However, exceptions are always there. The subject matter, in the following paragraphs, is the dynamics of some government interventions.

India, the abode of largest number of working children has relied on government initiatives through legislation and intervention by means of education, to tackle the problem of child labour. The country has a history of child labour legislation which goes back to 1881 when the first minimum age legislation was introduced. At that time employment of children under seven years of age was prohibited in factories. But this was a part of the Indian factories Act and not an exclusive legislation for working children. Such an Act was promulgated in 1938 as the Employment of Child Act prohibiting children under fifteen years in hazardous work. Then a spate of acts were introduced. However the culmination may be the Child Labour (Prohibition & Regulation) Act of 1986. As a complementary action, the same year a National Policy on Child Labour was enunciated to provide strength to the Act and also envisaging interventions in the social sector with a view to have the integrated development of child.

Government of India chose education as the main plank of its Policy and an ambitious project of creating half a million non-formal education centres was launched. It aimed at integrated child development and improvement in employment condition of working children.

Another major intervention programme was pilot action project for children working in hazardous industries such as match-making, carpet-weaving, glass manufacturing and gem-polishing with an initial objective of providing safe working condition, access to health and non-formal education facilities, with an initial, and gradually eliminating child labour as the long-term objective.

However, the implementation has been the weakest point and no objective of the intervention programme could be achieved in India due to financial and administrative lapses. It has also failed to enlist public support or in raising public awareness. Informal education could not catch up either with the targeted pupil or parents of working children. How the lack of political will and commitment can sabotage any programme and defeat the purpose may be judged from the implementation of the National Policy on Child Labour. Hence no tangible results. The theory stands good, conventions and thereby legislations exist but the practice defied whatever was supposed to be achieved. One step forward in terms of theory and convention brought one step backward in terms of practice, hence "zero-sum" game situation persists.

Education certainly proves a deterrent for child labour. The state of Kerala in India, where universal primary education has been most successful, has less incidence of child labour. It has been found that children's school retention from morning till afternoon in Kerala leaves not much scope for child labour. True that children work in coir and other industries in their spare time so their working hours are less and certainly not at the cost of education. It may be reminded here that the universal education programme in Kerala has not been implemented to check child labour. But the fact is that the universal education highly demanded by population itself has been an 'effect', and not the cause for child labour, and what Boyden and Myres[1] called, *workplace abuse of children has successfully been contained.* Investment in primary and basic education does pay in terms of preventing the abuse of child labour. Hence there is a strong case for universal education in developing countries and that too, as an intervention programme for gradual and long-term elimination of child labour and work place abuses.

NOTES

1. Boyden, J and William Myres (1999), *Exploring Alternative Approaches to Combating Child Labour: Case Studies from Developing Countries, Florence (Italy),* International Child Development Centre, UNICEF, p. 10.

2. CHILD LABOUR

Customarily child labour has been defined as the work being done by a child of less than fifteen years of age[1] with or without remuneration engaged in activities facilitating the work of adults and partially or wholly substituting any adult worker. In the case of households, nature of child work is facilitating as adults or even children of the employer become free for other activities commensurating their status, profession, age and experience. Whereas in other economic activities such as mending cattles, agriculture, petty trade, services, marginal manufacturing activities, child labour substitutes adult workers, if not wholly then partly.

Competition and reciprocity[2] both are invariably associated with the perception of child labour. It is either competing with adults selling goods on the streets, manufacturing or making articles in the informal sector or providing services to the community members. A child engaged in match-making for example, in Sivakashi[3] or making beedis (local cigarettes) in various parts of India like Medak[4] (Andhra Pradesh), Rampur (Uttar Pradesh) and Jabalpur (Madhya Pradesh), Carpets in Bhadoi (Mirzapur, UP), Varanasi[5] (U.P.), Shahjahanpur (U.P.), or in other countries like Nepal[6], Pakistan[7], Iran[8], Egypt[9] and Morocco[10] actually substitutes adult labour. Hand-knotted carpets are infamous for being made by child labour. Street vending children selling generally articles of daily consumption ranging from candies to kitchen wares are substituting adult vendors.

On the contrary, child working along with his father in the field, sowing, weeding and harvesting crop may be characterized as reciprocity. Similarly, gem polishing in Jaipur[11] (India), food selling in Kano[12] (Nigeria) and learning family crafts in almost all the south Asian countries fall in the reciprocity category of child work. Sometimes it becomes difficult to draw a line of demarcation between competition and reciprocity when, for example, a child acts as wage earner and also works along with his father in the family business or profession.

A common question, diluting the issue of child labour, has been : if a child gets a glass of water for his parents, is it child labour? It makes necessary to distinguish between 'work' and 'labour' done by a child. These concepts[13] are usually taken synonyms which raises problem. Every child during the course of physical and mental development does work. It is a normal activity of a child to learn about customs, traditions, manners depending upon the family background and the way in which children are brought up. Such activities or work are necessary for the social, mental and physical development of the child. All such things which a child learns and does are not bad since these do not stunt either social or psychological development. No society in the world considers such work bad and these are recognized in the rite of passage to adulthood. Moreover, work done by a child would not be at the cost of leisure, health, play and education. Nothing gets hampered, nothing is adverse for the development of child. On the contrary, labour is that work of the child depriving leisure, play and education, even impairing health and development. Hence a distinction should be made between child work and child labour where the former may be for the betterment while latter implies adverse to the development of a child. Schooling and home work invariably commensurate the age, physical and mental capabilities of the child and, hence, never treated as child labour; whereas carrying a load of bricks over the head or working in some sweatshop are always taken as child labour irrespective of the stage through which the society is passing. What, then distinguishes 'work' from 'labour' in the case of child? Common denominator may be exploitation if depriving leisure, play and education can be taken as its elements. Child labour if structured and phased properly may reduce its exploitative nature, however, could not get eliminated. This may be the reason forcing to advocate to study "the question of work on the basis of whether or not it constitutes exploitation. It is infact this idea which motivated the establishment of a study programme on child labour. The notion of exploitation can accommodate original concepts and hypotheses and an examination of the concrete mechanism behind the work of children..."[14]. At this juncture of literature development on child labour demarcation between 'child work' and 'child labour' seems to be appropriate.

So far two controversies have been resolved namely definitions of child and that of 'child labour'. Controversy seems to have arisen about the definition of child. Who is a child?[15], which criterion to be accepted for defining child . . . . (puberty) biological age, legal or custom?[16] Since definition given by the ILO has been accepted by member countries, controversy has subsided, if not eliminated. Susceptible to implementation aspect of biological age in the matter of prevention and elimination of child labour makes uneasy. The apprehension is that the child or poor families from where child labour orginates never know the birth year due to illiteracy. Who is, and how to determine the age? Well, question is valid but preciseness does not matter much. Thus the definition of child adopted and advocated by the ILO should not cause much discomfort to the antagonists.

Analogously, distinction between 'work' and 'labour' made on the basis of 'exploitation' has been widely accepted and provided, if not a full stop then, semi-colon to the controversy in this regard. However, once the element of 'exploitation' is introduced in the definition of child labour, it becomes a controversy in itself. What is exploitation in the case of child labour? This task is also not simple as aptly remarked that "..exploitation is not a concept that can be given a precise objective meaning".[18] Do we agree that the "exploitation will be in the eye of the beholder?"[19] To rest this controversy it may safely be presumed that anything which hampers social development of the child as per the existing norms of a society, may be treated as exploitation. Child labour certainly strains the child, physically, socially or psychologically, hence tantamounts to exploitation. Some sort of definition or explanation has to be considered to resolve this controversial aspect of child labour. Certain practices have to be eliminated which embody exploitation, such as, child prostitution, bonded and tied labour, work dangerous for health, child militants and soldiers in guerilla armies etc. The norms of civilized society, be in a developed or developing country, normally consider such factors exploitative. This is the simple reason for which consensus has developed among the countries of the world to eliminate child labour. Finding 'total' solution to a controversy acceptable to all may not be the objective, but solution to the problem, that is, child labour, certainly is.

Is child labour uniform in nature across a country? Simply not. It exists in varied forms and, hence, may be subjected to categorization. Now, question is what should be the criteria to categorise child labour? Infact, nature of engagement or activities has been considered as explicit factor to form various categories of child labour and that too, in a most generalized manner. However, the implicit factor which may be read between lines is exploitation. Hence child labour is usually linked with exploitation. There may be degrees of exploitation different in various occupations and socio-economic milieu. Its connotation may be positive or negative. In some activities exploitation of potential or capability is involved without any ulterior motives, such as baby-sitting at one's own home. Even in such cases straining of a child can not be ruled out. It is not for the sake of child but facilitating mother's responsibilities at home or at work. The categories may be listed in the following manner.[20]

In every society children do a number of work at their homes. Sometimes asked for baby-sitting, cleaning and help in cooking. On some occasions, child especially a female may be engaged in cooking. It has been a custom in south Asian societies to assign some of the household chores to the girls even at a tender age, to clean and cook regularly as it is considered necessary to 'prepare' the girls for their future life. Teenager girls

CHART 1

Child Labour—Non-domestic, Non-monetary

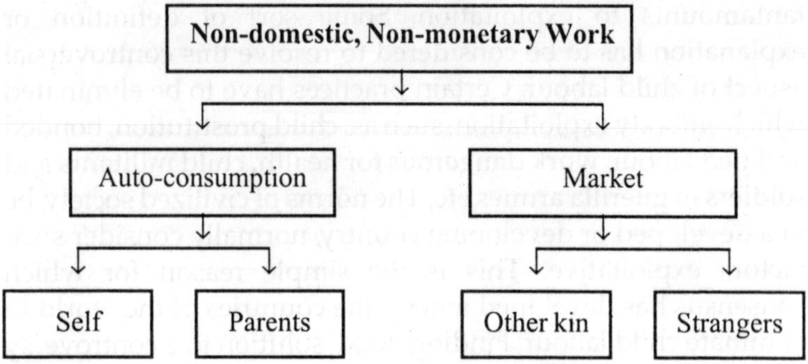

have to share more responsibilities of domestic chores as they grow. Boys are spared more for domestic work compared with girls due to customs and traditions. However, domestic work for children has a definite gender- bias in most of the societies. Even it persists where girls are relatively less burdened than boys. [21] In the oriental societies, rural and urban domestic work and other associated aspects are distinctly marked. It is generally rural female child who has to work for longer hours as compared to urban female child of the same age. In the case of domestic work of children, it is merely division of labour which actually leads to assignment of their work. However exploitative elements are not ruled out. The degree of exploitation may vary from mild to intense for the social, physical and psychological development of child, since domestic work is also at the cost of either leisure/ play or education of child.

NON-DOMESTIC (NON-MONETARY) CHILD LABOUR

Child work in subsistence economies is characterized by activities which fall under this category. Effort has been made to work out a division between 'work related to subsistence production' and 'work related to market production'. This is true in the case of rural area but situation in urban area slightly differs. However, the following pattern given by Rodgers and Standing[22] holds good:

This time-use breakdown of non-domestic, non-monetary work of children also has implicit exploitative element. Children mending one's own cattles, assisting father in agricultural activities particularly during sowing and harvesting times or helping in business such as running a shop do at the cost of their leisure, play and education. Just like domestic work, non-domestic, non-monetary work of child is also characterized by exploitative elements and even more intense. However, in both the activities child labour is of a facilitative rather than substitutive as adult labour is not fully replaced.

BONDED CHILD LABOUR

In fact this category of child labour has drawn attention of the scholars, social workers and international organization more than any other. South Asian countries like India, Pakistan, Bangladesh and Nepal, similarly south American, such as, Peru, Columbia and Brazil still can not claim to be free from bonded child labour in their economies.

The ILO Convention Concerning Forced or Compulsory Labour, 1930 defined it as "all work or service which is exacted from any person under the menace of any penalty and for which the said person has not offered himself voluntarily."[23] Bonded labour exists in different forms. India, for example, has it as socially pledged, tied due to economic reasons, forced because of social milieu. In any form, however, socio-economic factors particularly caste system plays the most important role. Servitude labour has its manifestation for children as well. Persons of low castes tied with the landlord belonging to upper caste were customarily forced to give their children in the service of landlord without any remuneration. Early fifties witnessed abolition of *Zamindari* (Landlord) system thus loosening the tie between servitude labour and landlords. But social milieu is changing at its own pace whereby caste system still trying to perpetuate 'force labour-tradition' of by gone era which has been abolished by the Bonded Labour System (Abolition) Act of 1976. Bihar in India is a classic example. Feudal system wherever prevailing still dodge the law enforcing agencies and system and makes effort to perpetuate forced labour.

In a highly referred paper[24] the case of bonded labour in India has been highlighted. The cases cited therein point towards 'pledged', 'tied' and 'bonded' child labour. The pledged child labour is the one where parents commit to sell the labour of their child for some favour, either in cash or kind. 'Tied' labour is usually secured by advancing some amount of money and, in turn, child gets tied with the secured loan. The worst form of child labour is 'bonded' labour-slavery like working condition. Child is forced to stay at the work site, sometimes guarded and rarely chained. Such working children are not allowed to move out of the premises and have to work for remuneration or without remuneration according to the sweet will of the employer. Slave like conditions exist and bonded labour awaits for the freedom[25] which they usually get due to the efforts of some NGOs[26]. Such child labour mostly comes from drought-prone areas of Bihar and Orissa infamous for their abject poverty.[27]

Bonded child labour has carved a niche in those industries which are generally in the interior areas. Classic example may be of brick-kilns employing large number of bonded labour.[28] A number of case studies have been collected on the use of forced and bonded child labour.[29]

CHILD WAGE LABOUR

Child Wage Labour category merits attention as majority of working children fall under this category. Child labour on daily wage is a common phenomenon, particularly in agricultural sector, in India. It is not tantamount to say that the other sectors are ruled out. In construction industry similar situation exists in most of south Asian countries. Unskilled workers including juveniles gather at specific places in every city to be hired on daily wages. Wage employment for children working in shops, restaurants and service trades is regular and usually not on daily wages. When the whole family is hired for agricultural work, than young children are part and parcel of family labour. It points out that the nature of wage employment differs even for children and is compatible with adult workers. In India, Pakistan and other developing countries wage employment pattern for working children is similar and may be classified into: (*i*) regular employment, (*ii*) casual/daily wage employment, and (*iii*) family package seasonal employment.

However, piece-rate and time-rate employment also prevail in certain sectors, especially for child labour. The common example of piece-rate employment in India and Pakistan is brick-making, match-making and other handicrafts such as embroidery. In such activities where piece-rate system prevails, time binding is absent. In northern part of India, embroidery centres, e.g., Delhi, Bareilly, Rampur, Lucknow and Bhopal piece-rate employment is common. Whatever, be the nature of child wage employment, remuneration is invariably less than the adult workers and even they have to strive for legal minimum wages. Child worker gets any thing between one-third and two-third of adult worker's wage. Exploitation of child wage workers is evident and blatant.

Another child work having the most exploitative nature is apprentice-ship. All the sweatshops, e.g., workshops, be it metal, wood or repairing and automobile garages employ apprentices of tender age, ranging between five and fifteen years. These children 'learn' skills for a number of years without any remuneration. Their working conditions are harsh in the sense that they have to do all the odd jobs. Sometimes weekly off-day is also denied to them. Automobile workshops are good example where a child worker has to come earlier than others in the morning to sweep and clean the work place. During the day, young child has to run at the beck and call of everyone. While in the evening the child worker is supposed to collect every tool and other things scattered in the open and inside the shop and has to arrange. Hence child worker comes first and goes last every day. It stretches working hours of child labour. They are also subjected to physical punishment for their mistakes and sometimes even without any mistake! Ill-treatment of such working children is the rule of the day and it goes on for years. Very occasionally they are given some paltry sum, especially around the festivals.

Is child wage labour is compatible with schooling or competitive? Answer to this question depends upon a number of factors, such as, location of work place, school in the vicinity, type of employment, perception of schooling in the family of child labour etc. It is certainly competitive if the employment is regular, say work in shops and workshops including garages does not permit for schooling of child labour. Agricultural work also employs child worker for a day of nine to eleven hours. Seasonal nature of job does not allow schooling for a certain period. Casual nature of employment gives certain degree of freedom for schooling. On all off days, child worker is free to attend the school.

However, piece-rate child workers may have schooling as compatible or complementary. Child workers in handicrafts or other family profession adjust their timings of work with that of school. It is common sight at embroidery centres that child worker goes to the school and does work in the free hours. Burra's well quoted paper[30] indicates compatibility with schooling in the Gem industry. Hence, irregular, casual and seasonal child wage employment are compatible with schooling, that too, to a certain degree. But regular and permanent wage employment deprives a child worker of education as this type of employment is essentially competitive to schooling. Again exploitation of child labour is very pronounced in the case of wage employment as the working child has to forego education, partly or wholly.

CHILD MARGINAL ECONOMIC ACTIVITY LABOUR

Large number of children in every developing country is engaged in such activities like newspaper selling, vending on the streets, car-washing and watching, selling food, shoe-shining and 'rag-picking' which are known as marginal economic activities. Child labour engaged in all these activities is substantial in all developing countries without exception. This category may be barring few activities, called self-employed child labour as most of working children 'own' their business. Selling of newspaper is generally an exception where child labour is hired on nominal wage, called commission, to sell newspaper on the streets, crossings and pavements. On the contrary, car-washing and watching, ragpicking and shoe-shining invariably fall under the head of child self-employment. The distribution of child marginal economic activity labour may be guessed from that most of the children work in services.[31]

The exploitation of child labour engaged in marginal economic activities is not ruled out since these children have to sell their articles and services at prices less than market prices. Car owner pay less than half of what they have to pay in a garage. Sometimes child who has washed the car is not paid since was not 'assigned' the job! Time-use data, if obtained then share of earnings would be less in comparison of their shares of total work time[32]. In may be taken as an indicator of exploitative mechanism prevailing in the system.

It may be observed that categorization or classification of child labour has been based on activities performed by working children under different socio-economic milieu. It means, thereby, lack of theoretical foundation to properly establish these categories. Thus generalization of such categories in the context of varied socio-economic situation becomes cumbersome and full of ambiguities. Conceptualisation in standard theoretical framework disappears the moment situation based analysis approach is being followed. Child labour is such a subject still awaiting theorization capable of being interpreted in terms of generalization.

How to recognize child labour? Are these specific or distinct characteristics attributable to child labour? The subject has been treated by scholars in a different manner. However, the object is the same. Not only the object but objective is also similar, that is, specification of child labour characteristics which may be a foundation of further analysis such as, distinguishing child labour from adult labour and, probing into exploitative mechanism invariably associated with child labour, etc.

The supply of child labour in a developing and populated country is 'infinite' due to high birth rate and high emigration from rural to urban centres. High birth rate coupled with low death rate increases juvenile population. The traditional bastions of child labour employment are agricultural sector in rural area and informal sector in urban centres. Agricultural sector being either subsistence or less developed and labour-oriented operates on low cost and hence has ever increasing demand for cheap labour, that is, child labour. In the case of subsistence agriculture, family labour is generally engaged and has a niche for child labour as it survives on low cost of low-level production. This 'low-cost-low-production' creates a space for child labour. Where as labour-oriented agricultural production also thrives on low cost of production for which it hires cheap labour, i.e., child labour.

On the other hand, large scale unemployment in developing countries makes a room for self-employment which, in turn, gives rise to informal sector. This sector is characterized by intensive competition and thus bound to keep its cost and price very low. Once again the 'low cost- low price' phenomenon creates demand for cheap labour, i.e., child labour.

While the supply of child labour in these two sectors goes on increasing due to widening gap between birth-death rates and rural-urban migration. The juvenile population is more in the urban centres as compared with rural sector.

Another characteristic distinguishing child labour from adult labour is the 'right to work'. In every developing and developed country children *per se* have no right to work due to national laws motivated largely by international conventions such as U.N. Convention[33], ILO Convention[34]. Consequently, children under fifteen years of age have generally been prohibited from working on regular basis for the sake of their physical and mental development. However, such legal provisions made the child labour more vulnerable as their employment and regularity are not governed or protected by the law of the country concerned but by the "unpredictable ebb and flow of orders and markets."[35] Van Hear [36] has presented this aspect in a very convincing manner.

Thirdly, intimidation of child labour such as, dismissal is extremely easy. Illegality of working children forbids them to form any organization or trade union to protect their interest. Hence, working children are always "subject to intimidation"[37].

The ILO has emphatically stated that logically children should not work at all, it follows that there can be no question of organizing them in unions.[38] Of course, children are working in millions all over the world and are always at the mercy of their employers who know that employment of children is not legal and hence dismiss them whenever they are not required. Neither employment is legal nor dismissal is illegal.

Fourthly, 'little hands' are particularly well suited conventionally for certain tasks such as hand-knotted carpets manufactured in India, Pakistan, Nepal, Iran, Egypt and Morocco etc., tobacco and match industries in the Indian sub-continent; jasmine flower picking in Egypt[39]. Thus certain tasks are believed to be well suited, technically and economically, to children so that child labour for specific work is distinguished from adult labour.

Fifthly, children have certain "physical and psychological characteristics such as agility, running and hiding, the ability to keep quite or to misled"[40] making them different from adults.

However, the ILO has identified the following characteristics of child labour:

- "Working too young—children in developing countries often start factory work at the age of six or seven;
- Working under strain—physical, social or psychological, in mines for example, or sweatshops;
- Working on the streets—or in unhealthy and dangerous conditions;
- For very little pay—as little as $3 for a 60 hour week;
- With little stimulation—dull or repetitive tasks, which stunt the child's social and psychological development;
- Taking too much responsibility—children often have charge of siblings only a year younger than themselves;
- Subject to intimidation—which inhibits self- confidence and self-esteem as with slave labour and sexual exploitation."[41]

These characteristics are however, typological and based on observation rather than theorization. Out of these, many may be applicable for adult labour in unorganized sector. A casual agricultural worker has to work from 6 a.m. to 6.30 p.m. in Indian villages, hence, working for long hours could not be ascribed to child labour as the specific characteristic. Similarly, a large number of adults work on the street in unhealthy and dangerous conditions. So nothing special about the child labour as the adults working on the street face all the health hazards and have to bear the weather vagaries. 'For very little pay' adults work, as ad-hoc employees, casual agricultural labourers where their wage for the whole week is even less than $ 3! Such adult workers like casual labourers; agricultural labourers are also subject to intimidation. Hence, specific characteristics of child labour should be distinct than what enumerated by the ILO. These should also have an input of theorization for the purpose of generalization. The 'infinite' supply of child labour has (following Lewis' terminology), for example, potential of generalization as well as theoretical input. Analogously, demand for child labour is elastic in the sense that higher the wage rate for child workers less the demand for child labour and its vice-versa.

Substitution or complementary elements may also be taken as characteristics of child labour, of course subject to the nature of work. Child labour in household sector is substitute in most of the situations. It can work for adult labour. While subsistence farming uses child labour as complementary. Hence the elasticities in these cases would be different from each other and also different vis-à-vis adult labour. In the informal sector, child labour may be substitute as well complementary for adult subject to: (*i*) nature of activity, (*ii*) level of skill required, and (*iii*) lagged adjustment between trainees and trained. The nature of activity, for example, vendors on the street are substitute, that is, activity may not be hampered if child labour takes it over. Selling candies, newspapers, flowers and other articles by children actually substitute adult vendors. Similarly, shoe-shining by working children leads to replacement of adult shoe-shiners. Skill factor also plays a very important role in replacing and not replacing adult workers. The substitution of adult by child labour is possible if skill is not required. However, for skilled workers child labour may not be a substitute. Time lag between apprentice-skilled worker largely determines replacement of adult by child labour in professions in which skill is a pre-requisite. During the lagged period, child labour could be complementary as it simply facilitate the work and augments productivity of adult labour. In the case of trade services child labour usually acts as complementary. The aforesaid determinants are important and should be taken into consideration. Since case studies and work of child labour have been taken for enumeration of characteristics, a fallacy seems to have been committed.

CAUSATIVE FACTORS

Economics not only revolves around demand and supply but also concentrates on causal chain of any social phenomenon to diagnose it. Modern economics has not confined itself to only economic factors but its domain covers socio-economic issues such as hunger, poverty and, famines, social choice by a host of economists including recent nobel laureate Amartya Sen. Since the days of Pareto may be earlier welfare economics came into existence dealing various economic issues in social context. In an analogous manner, child labour should not be mistaken as social or anthropological issue as economics being a social science has its share in riding over rough-shods. Each stream viz. sociology, politics, anthropology and economics has to play its role, not as substitutive but complementarity nature should be strengthened in order to find a solution to this complex problem of human being as well as humanity. The complexity of the problem of child labour needs an approach capable of not only trajecting but also uprooting. Causative approach to the problem may lead to better comprehension which, in turn, opens the door for interventions aiming at complete eradication. However, it is not as simple as a priori it seems. In large number of countries political will lacks which has *de facto* washed away all socio-economic and legal measures.

A simplistic approach to analyse the problem could be listing all the factors responsible for the demand for and supply of child labour, without dealing with their intricacies. Such a list is generally given in all the sociological, anthropological studies, and official reports such as the one prepared by the U.S. Department of Labour[42]. It should not be taken as reflection as it is because of the scope and nature of these studies and reports the reasons generally listed for the demand for child labour are: large availability of children in rural areas; children draw their earnings or livelihood from other farms or plantation, low wage rate as compared with adult worker and, more docile and pliant nature of working children[43]. On the supply of child labour poverty, educational factors, societal attitudes, minority status and government policy[44] are given. Nothing is wrong about out lining factors for demand and supply, except that causal chain or analysis is missing. However, the same can not be said about other studies such as by Rodgers and Standing[45] and Schildkrout[46] etc. However, theorization may be from another angle which could shed some more light on theoretical grey areas of the subject.

The supply of child labour is abundant in any developing country. But why? Is it different from the conventional notion of supply which is in turn, expressed as $S=f(P)$, where dependent variable, i.e. supply is a direct function of price? How supply of child labour can be expressed?

Let us first take up the first issue, that is, sources of the supply of child labour in any country. The first determinant is the birth rate. Higher the birth rate, coupled with low death rate, higher the supply of child labour. Does it mean that the supply of child labour is irrespective of price? Or supply of child labour is not a function of price? Does not it seems contradictory that supply of child labour is abundant or plentiful and supply is a function of price? Once supply is taken as a function of price, it can be plentiful only when price is very high. Why is there ambiguity? The simple reason is that the availability and supply notions are not being distinguished. When birth rate is high than the death rate, juvenile population is bound to increase. Since birth rate is invariably high in all the developing countries, there is plentiful availability of children which may, due to socio-economic reason, turn into child labour. On the other hand, supply of child labour is not only a function of high birth or emigration rate but also has price factor involved in it. Abundant availability of children in a developing country makes possible plentiful supply of child labour and this depresses price factor in the labour market. However, the relationship between supply of child labour and price may not be negated. The availability is biological phenomenon while supply is socio-economic phenomenon. Higher the birth rate, larger would be the size of child population. But supply of child labour would be higher when wage rate is higher. Hence establishment of functional relationship is necessary if ambiguity of notions is to be dispensed with. Moreover, economic analysis deviates here from sociological analysis. The supply of child labour has to be analysed in terms of functional relationship if child labour is to be studied in the context of labour market, be it for the household sector, agriculture or informal sector. If no interventions are considered then

$$S_{CL} = f(P)$$

Where S_{CL}, P stand for supply of child labour and its price respectively. Now the availability of child labour may be expressed as $A = f(R_b, R_e, ---)$ where A, R_b & R_e stand for availability, birth rate, emigration rate..... If the rates of birth and emigration are high, larger would be the availability of children which may lead to large child labour force in the market.

In the case of supply of child labour why its prices i.e. wage is not as strong factor as it is for the supply of adult labourer? The reasons are many. Some of these are: availability is plentiful, little bargaining power due to absence of organization or union which is, in turn, due to legal reasons, intensely competitive environment. The market for child labour is basically a buyer's market and not like seller's market of adult workers. Hence, it becomes a distinguishing point where a line of demarcation between child labour and adult labour may be drawn, that too, with respect to the supply. Adult labour is protected by legal and socio-economic institution. It has laws governing wages, working hours and other working condition, beside trade unions to protect the interest of adult workers. On the contrary, legal provisions aim at eliminating child labour and there can not be any organization or union to safeguard their interests as child labour. This makes the child labour market a buyer's market which is capable of imposing its conditions on child labourers and hence its price, i.e., wage a determinant of supply is 'depressed'.

To conclude arguments, supply of child labour depends on a number of socio-economic factors, such as, high birth and migration rates, which induce the supply of child labour, its price or wage rate, which is depressed as a result of large availability of working children, intensely competitive environment and no bargaining power. However, supply of child labour is a function of wage rate. Thus a distinction between availability and supply is necessitated. This particular factor has been over looked in most of the studies.

The determinants of the supply of child labour may be broadly categorized into two: (*i*) autonomous and, (*ii*) induced. The autonomous is defined which is irrespective of demand and other factors. In case of child labour supply, autonomous factor is growth rate of population. i.e., gap between birth and death rates. It is technically speaking, not high birth rate but population growth rate which makes labour supply plentiful. Moreover, high population growth rate leading to plentiful supply of child labour is autonomous as it does not depend upon the level of socio-economic development or demand factor. Hence, the axiom may be.

Higher the population growth rate, larger the supply of child labour.

Thus taking the population growth rate autonomous, supply of child labour becomes the function of wage rate. However, plentiful supply of child labour shall determine a lower wage rate, provided that demand for child labour falls short of plentiful supply. Figure 1 explains determination of wage. The supply curve taken as the function of wage, moves towards horizontal shape considering the plentiful nature of child labour supply or infinite supply, lowers wage rates.

Larger is the supply of children, lower is the wage rate.

Other determinants of child labour supply are induced factors which actually enforce the growth of supply. Among the

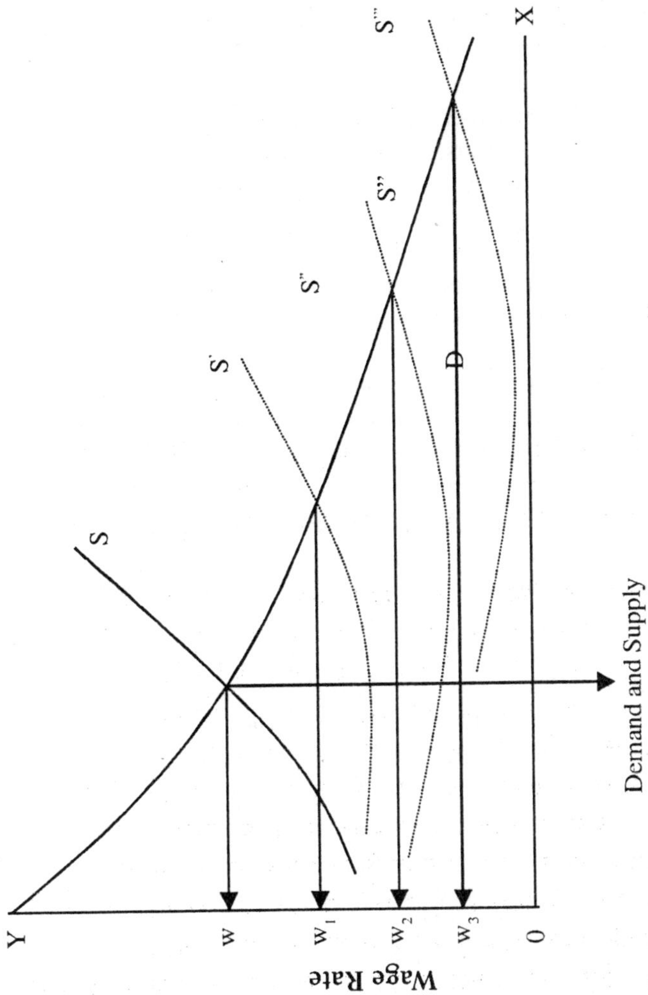

FIGURE 1

induced determinants of supply, most important is poverty, which is the root cause of the supply of child labour in any developing country. Most of the socio-economic problems have stemmed from poverty. So is the child labour.

Poverty has many facets or dimensions and hence, has different notions such as economic poverty which is further classified into absolute poverty and relative poverty; social poverty; cultural poverty and even aesthetical poverty! Which notion of poverty has to be taken into account in the context of child labour? The socio-economic concept of poverty potentially covers major dimensions, such as, production and productivity, education, nutrition, cultural factors like family, traditions and customs. Thus socio-economic concept of poverty serves the purpose of dealing with child labour.

The poverty as a concept is reflected in 'deprivations' of basic needs, that is, lack of means to fulfil basic needs or minimum needs of a family for private consumption[48] such as, food, clothing and housing without which survival is not possible. There is always a 'critical minimum' necessary for the survival of a person, be it a minor or major. The 'critical minimum' may vary from person to person and also differs from place to place. What is critical minimum in a village may fall short of that in a city. However, efforts have been made to specify the basic requirements in urban and rural settings in every country to define poverty. In India, for example, poverty line has been defined in terms of economic parameters so as to identify poors living below the poverty line. Similar attempts must have been made in other developing countries as per their socio-economic context. In certain terms can be said that the 'vicious circle of poverty' exists in developing countries which perpetuates poverty and hence interventions are required. For example, Government of India launched poverty eradication programme and now the world feeling concerned has the World Poverty Eradication Day! The purpose is to highlight the issue of suffering and plight of the poor so as to alleviate it, if eradication is not possible in the present circumstances existing in the countries of the Third World.

The 'vicious circle of poverty' may be explained as given in

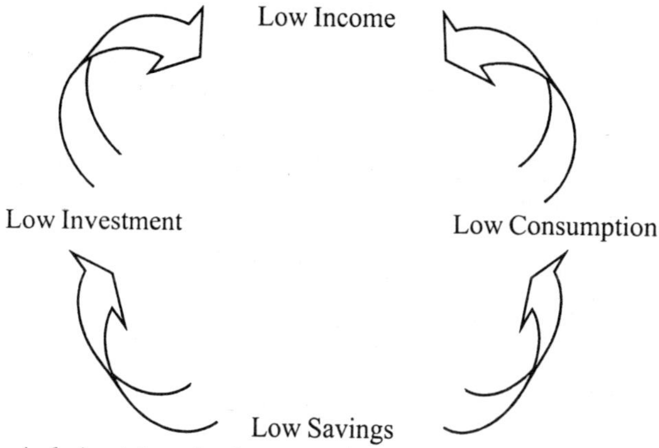

This circle is vicious in the sense that it can not be broken easily.

the elementary text book:

This circle is vicious in the sense that it can not be broken easily. The economy remains, using Nelson's terminology, in the low equilibrium trap. A 'big push' is required which is generally beyond the means of a developing country. Hence, vicious circle of poverty persists. But how to co-relate child labour with the poverty? The dynamics of poverty makes it possible. A simplistic way is to begin with the poor- one who is living below the poverty as determined by the government of a country. Since birth rate is high, size of the family is large. Income is not sufficient to meet the basic needs. Child goes to work to supplement the family income hence basic needs are fulfilled. Since child labour aims at supplementary wage to supplement meagre income of the bread earner, it is invariably low. Moreover, there is intensive competition in the labour market due to plentiful supply of child labour which is, in turn because of high growth rate of population. This, poor ⇒ large family ⇒ high birth rate ⇒ plentiful supply of child labour ⇒ low wage ⇒ poor, circular reasoning completes the circle. But intention is to highlight that child labour perpetuates poverty. Whatsoever, be the nature of poverty, it eventually induces child labour in poor country. Hence, poverty is a great inducement for child labour leading to supply of child labour in proportion to poverty.

More is the poverty in a country, larger is the supply of child labour. For example, India and Bangladesh both are poor but Bangladesh in relatively more poor than India. By logic Bangladesh must have a large percentage of child workers than India. In the Eightees, Bangladesh had child labour force as 2.1% of its population, while India had it only 1.5%[47]. Again it is circular reasoning of course, but has the potential to drive home the point. Hence, axiom may be :

More is the poverty, larger is the supply of child labour.

Another factor inducing supply of child labour is educational system in a country. There is *a priori* inverse relation between supply of child labour and school facilities where the former gets curtailed when the latter expands. The provision of compulsory basic education is supposed to reduce the supply of child labour. It is believed that the "education laws are the best child labour laws"[49].

Ofcourse, there is a nexus between child labour and basic education. The enforcement of compulsory basic education laws largely curtail and eventually eliminate child labour. Moreover, it is relatively easy to enforce school laws than child labour laws in the sense that inspectorate of the latter can never be as large so as to inspect widely dispered units of child employment, while the school network can easily do it.

The instrument of compulsory elementary education may also be used selectively in a state or region where child labour is a menace. If, for example, child labour is employed to the maximum in the urban informal sector, compulsory education introduced in such urban areas would drastically cut the size of child labour force. In any case, augmentation of school facilities will adversely affect child labour provided that its aim is to serve the poorest of the poor. The axiom, therefore, is:

Scarce the basic education, abundant the supply of child labour.

Cultural factors also induce the supply of labour in a poor country. These factor, such as, societal attitude, customs and traditions all affect the choice of parents and thereby choice of children. In those societies where very few believe in basic education, child labour gets promoted [50]. In poor families in Southeast Asian countries parents believe in training their very young children in trade services, such as, mechanics so that they start earning at a young age. In the meantime these working children are expected to supplement meagre family income. Certain socio-economic backward communities especially minorities[51] for example, muslim community in India, has an indifferent attitude towards education; poor families of this community largely send their children to garages and other trade services for apprentice ship so that their children learn some skill and supplement family income. Such an attitude contributes in increasing the supply of child labour.

Nomadic society, as in Africa, is governed by its own customs and traditions which encourage child labour "Indeed, from the age of seven, children are involved in economic activities..."[52] and children get engaged in activities as per their gender. The same is true about 'vana-gujjars' or goojers in India. Similarly in agricultural activities boys work for preparing, sowing, clearing and surveilling fields and harvesting crops while girls assist in sowing, surveillance and harvesting. What Dawson states as reasons for the failure of educational project for the nomads of Somalia, also throws light on their attitude, that is, reluctance to change their traditional way of life and parents do not relieve their children from the responsibilities of tending the flocks.[53] If perception is not changed, as noticed in the case of Masai in Kenya, child labour could be preferred over education.[54] All these empirical studies and observations in developing country point out that cultural factors induce the supply of child labour if societal attitude and perceptions are not changed. In some societies like Indonesia the cultural values not only accept but also encourage child employment as an educational process[55]. The axiom, hence, may be expressed as:

More is traditionally backward society, more is child labour.

Lack of political will to eliminate child labour has also induced the supply of child labour. In most of the Third World countries, policies have been drafted to ban child labour but implementation or enforcement of law is so poor as if policies are non-existent. Hence the growth of child labour is unabated. Whatever child labour abolition laws are implemented these affect only a fraction of child labour force and, that too, in the urban sector only. Since rural and informal sectors are overlooked by the law enforcing agencies, these sectors have large supply of child labour. Government's lukewarm attitude towards banning child labour reflecting lack of political will has induced the supply of child labour not only in the agricultural and household sectors but, to some extent, in the informal sector as well.

The axiom may be stated as:

Lack of political will and poor enforcement of law induce supply of child labour.

One of the most important factor inducing the supply of child labour is rural-urban migration. Growing industrialization and urbanization are the two usual determinants of migration from rural areas to urban centres. The urban sector in a developing country has better living and employment opportunities as compared with rural side. It attracts the landless, manual workers and other unemployed in the villages. These families of poors and unemployed get settled in urban cities where growing industrialization and expanding informal sector offer them employment opportunities. Children belonging to these families of poor, unemployed and landless labourers migrated from the country side get work avenues in garages, workshops, street vending and other activities in the informal sector. Thus the migration from rural to urban centres, as inducement, leads to ever growing supply of child labour in urban and industrial centres.

All the industrial centres are known for developing ancillary units in and around the city. Similarly, nuclii also develop satellite towns buzzing with activities of ancillary units. These generally lead to *sub-contracting system* which, in turn, encourage child labour in the sub-contracting units. Hence, cost-conscious low production sub-contracting and other ancillary units become harbingers of child labour. Thus,

Higher the emigration rate, larger the supply of child labour.

To conclude the supply of child labour it may be stated that it has two aspects *viz.* autonomous supply and induced supply. The autonomous supply of child labour is due to the high birth-rate in a country. Higher the birth-rate or growth-rate of population, larger would be the autonomous supply of child labour. This kind of supply is described as autonomous since it does not depend upon either the level of development or demand. It is irrespective of a corresponding factor such as wage-rate. Simply expands with time, population and, hence

$$S_{CLA} = f\,(t,p)$$

that is, autonomous supply of child labour is a function of population size and time.

Whereas induced supply of child labour is because of certain socio-economic and cultural factors, such as, poverty, rural-urban migration, education, societal attitude and perception about child labour etc. Thus,

$$S_{CLi} = f\,(s,c,e,..)$$

Where the induced supply of child labour depends upon social, cultural and economic,...., factors. Conceptually the total supply of child labour may depend upon the autonomous and induced factors however, these may vary from place to place.

In conventional economics, demand is expressed as a function of price, *other things being the same,*

$$D = f\,(P)$$

Ofcourse, price is the most important factor influencing demand. Does the same relation exists between the demand for child labour and wage-rate? Is the wage-rate only factor determining demand for child labour? If not so, what are other socio-economic determinants of demand for child labour? Once these issues are settled and demand determinants are delineated, another question may need attention. What type of demand for child labour may be?

Let us begin with the determinants of demand for child labour in a general set-up rather than in some specific sectors' setting. Child labour is mainly employed on account of its cheapness in terms of price, i.e., demand for child labour is primarily a function of wage-rate

$$D_{CL} = f(w)$$

Where D_{CL} and w stand for demand for child labour and wage rate respectively. The demand equation shows an inverse relation between child labour and wage-rate. It, however, fails to explain the reason that why the wage for child labour remains low as compared with that of adult worker. This may, perhaps, be taken as a characteristic capable of distinguishing between demand for child labour and demand for adult labour. One of the obvious reason is plentiful supply of child labour which keeps its wage at a low level. Secondly, illegality of child labour depresses its price, i.e., wage-rate. This factor in particular makes it the 'buyer's' market and not 'seller's' market meaning that employers are in a position to determine the wage-rate and child worker has no choice. It is a sort of 'take-it or leave-it' situation. From the illegality aspect of child labour another characteristic stems, that is, child labour can have no organization, union or association. It clearly reflects on its bargaining power which is non-existent due to absence of union. Hence, market for child labour is governed by the employers and not by the sellers. In such a situation, perpetuating in every economy, wages for child labour are always 'depressed' and low vis-à-vis adult worker. However, physical characteristic of child labour and societal attitude about child labour also lead to low wage-rates. Physically child is not as strong as a mature person, and hence this societal attitude keeps wage-rate of child labour at a low level. Therefore, reasons for low wages for child labour are mainly social, pertaining to perceptions and attitudes, rather than economic, i.e., large supply.

Other determinants of demand for child labour are social, physical or traditional such as customs. Child labour is also demanded because it is docile and more pliant.[56] Similarly, demand for child labour sometimes depends on "children's physical and psychological characteristics, such as agility, running and hiding, the ability to keep quite or to mislead"[57] which are needed for clandestine and illegal work.

Child labour is also demanded for physical characteristics

and also due to traditions. Certain tasks such as match-making, beedi-making are technically well suited to children and highly profitable from the point of view of the employers[58] hence "little hands" have a large demand. Cultural factors or traditions also create demand for child labour and the classic example is demand for child labour in the carpet industry in every carpet manufacturing country in the Third World. Traditions *per se* determine demand for child labour.

Demand for child labour, may be due to its complexity, has not been discussed in much of the existing literature. Specifically in terminology of economics, demand for child labour, on *ceteris paribus* assumption, may be stated as

$$D_{CL} = f(W)$$

that is demand for child labour is a function of wage-rate. Since wage rate by nature of the supply of child labour remains low, demand for child labour keeps growing, subject to the condition that there are no interventions.

However, the nature of demand for child labour would be generally elastic in the sense that higher the wage-rate lower would be the demand, though this is over simplistic view. Demand for child labour also gets affected by the wage-rate of adult workers. If the gap between child and adult wage-rates becomes very narrow, adult workers get preference and hence demand for child labour goes down. On the contrary if adult wage rate, because of minimum wage fixed by the government, is high and child wage rate due to plentiful supply and lack of unionization is quite low, then the demand for child labour would go up. Here comes the concept of cross elasticity of demand. Hence, demand for child labour has a high cross elasticity of demand, that is, when the 'price' of adult labour goes up it will increase the demand for child labour. Even increased demand for child labour may not lead to increase in its 'price' due to plentiful nature of the supply. It also distinguishes demand for child labour from demand for adult labour.

REFERENCES

1. ILO (1973), *Minimum Age for Admission to Employment,* ILO, Article 2 Sec 3 of C 138, Minimum Age Convention, 1973.

2. Morice, A (1981), "The Exploitation of Children in the 'Informal Sector': Proposals for Research", in Gerry Rodgers and Guy Standing (eds.) *Child work, Poverty and Under development,* Geneva, ILO, p. 150.
3. Kuklarni, M.N. "Match-making children in Sivakasi", *Economic and Political Weekly,* XVIII, 43, Pp. 185-6.
4. Marla, S. (1977), "Bonded labour in Medak District, A.P." *NLI Bulletin,* 3: 10, pp. 424 & 430.
5. Gangrade, KD. & A. J. Gathia (1983), *Women and Child Workers in the Unorganised Sector,* New Delhi, Concept House Publishing Co.
6. Sattaur, O. (1993), *Child Labour in Nepal,* Kathmandu, Child Workers in Nepal Concerned Center.
7. Hafeez, S. (1979), *Child Labour in Pakistan,* Geneva, ILO (mimeo).
8. Challis, J &D Elliman (1979), *Child Workers Today,* Middlesex, Quartermaine House Ltd., pp. 55-6.
9. Fergany, N. (1993), *Child Labour in the Arab Countries,* The Arab Council for Childhood and Development, as quoted in U.S. Deptt of Labour, *By the Sweat & Toil of Children,* Washington D.C., July 15, 1994, Pp. 62-3.
10. Anti-Slavery Society (1978), *Child Labour in Morocco's Carpet Industry,* London (mimeo).
11. Burra, N. (1988) "Exploitation of Children in Jaipur Gem Industry: Health Hazards of Gem Polishing", *Economic & Political Weekly,* Jan. 23, pp. 135-6.
12. Schildkrout, E. (1981), "The Employment of Children in Kano (Nigeria)", in Gerry Rodgers & Guy Standing (eds.), *Op. cit.,* pp. 81-112.
13. Fyfe, A. (1989), *Child Labour,* Oxford, Polity Press, esp. pp. 3-5.
14. Morice, A (1981), *op. cit.,* p. 136.
15. Fyfe, A. (1995), "Child Labour" in Judith Ennew (ed.), *Learning or Labouring*? Florence, International Child Development Centre, UNICEF, p. 13.
16. Morice, A (1981), *op. cit.,* p. 136.
17. ILO (1973), *op. cit.*
18. Fyfe, A. (1995), *op. cit.*
19. *Ibid*, p. 14.
20. Rodgers, G. & G. Standing (1981), "The Economic Roles of Children : Issues for Analysis", in Gerry Rodgers & Guy Standing (eds.), *op. cit.,* pp. 2-11.
21. *Ibid*, p.2.
22. *Ibid*, p.4.
23. ILO (1930), *Convention Concerning Forced or Compulsory Labour,* C 29, Geneva, Article 2.
24. Burra, N. (1986), "Child labour in India: Poverty, Exploitation and Vested Interest", *Social Action,* 36, pp. 248-50.
25. ILO (1992), *Children in Bondage,* Geneva, ILO.
26. U.S. Deptt. of Labour (1994), *op. cit.,* cited Bonded Labour Liberation

Front, Mirzapur, ff 28, p. 77.
27. Burra, N. (1995), "Child Bonded Labourers in India", Judith Ennew (ed.), *op. cit.*, p. 71.
28. Mahmood, Z. et. al. (1991), *Child Labour in Brick-kiln Industries,* Lahore University of Punjab.
29. U.S. Deptt. of Labour (1995), *By the Sweat & Toil of Children,* Vol II. The Use of Child labour in U.S. Agricultural Imports & Forced and Bonded Child Labour, Washington D.C, Bureau of International Labour Affairs, esp. pp 77-149.
30. Burra, N. (1988), "Exploitation of Children in Jaipur Gem Industry II: Health Hazards of Gem Polishing", *Economic & Political Weekly,* Jan. 23, pp. 135-6.
31. Schibotte, G. & A. Cussianovich (1994), *Working Children; Building an Identity,* Lima Peru, Manthoc, p. 66.
32. Rosenzweing, M.R. (1981), "Household and Non-household Activities of Youth: Issues of Modeling, Data and Estimation Strategies", in G. Rodgers & G. Standing (eds.), *op. cit.,* p. 233.
33. U.N. (1989), *Convention on the Rights of the Child,* Article 32, sections (1) & (2) especially sub-section 2(a).
34. ILO (1973), *Recommendation Concerning Minimum Age for Admission to Employment,* Geneva, esp. section-II on Minimum Age of section-IV, On Conditions of Employment.
35. Morice, A (1981), *op. cit.,* p. 144.
36. Van Hear, N. (1982), "Child Labour and the Development of Capitalist Agriculture in Ghana", *Development and Change,* 13:4, pp. 499-514.
37. ILO (1992), "From Work to Exploitation", *World Labour Report,* Geneva, ILO, p. 14.
38. ILO (1996), *Trade Unions and Child Labour,* 102, Geneva, ILO, pp.3-4.
39. U.S. Deptt. of Labour (1995), *By the Sweat & Toil of Children,* Vol II, Washington D.C., Bureau of International Labour Affairs, p. 41.
40. Morice, A. (1981), *op. cit.,* p. 145.
41. ILO (1992), "*From work to exploitation*" in Ennew, J. (ed.), *Learning or Labouring?,* Florence, ICDC (UNICEF), 1995, p. 14.
42. U.S. Deptt. of Labour (1995), *By the Sweat & Toil of Children,* Vol II, Washington, D.C., Bureau of International Labour Affairs, pp. 25-30.
43. *Ibid*, p. 25.
44. *Ibid*, pp. 26-30.
45. Rodgers, G. & G. Standing (1981), *op. cit.,* pp. 1-45, esp. Section II.
46. Schildkrout, E. (1981), *op. cit.,* pp. 81-106, exp. pp 99-105.
47. Ennew, J and B. Milne (1989), *The Next Generation : Lives of Third World Countries,* London, Zed Books, Table 6, p. 74 (computed from table).
48. de Bernis, G.D. (1986), "Basic Needs and Dynamics of Development", in JASPA (ed.), *The Challenge of Employment & Basic Needs in Africa,* Nairobi, OUP, p. 30.

49. Fyfe, A. (1989), *op. cit.*, pp. 15-16.
50. Weiner, M. (1991), *The Child and the State in India*, Princeton, OUP, esp. pp. 191-196.
51. U.S. Deptt. of Labour (1975), *op. cit.*, p. 29.
52. Kane, A. Salan (1995), "The Work of Child Nomads", in J. Ennew (ed.), *op. cit.*, p. 68.
53. Dawson, G.D. (1964), "Education in Somalia", *Comparative Education Review*, No. 8., p. 201.
54. Lavers, A. (1960), "Schooling in Massailand", *Kenya Education Journal*, No. 1.
55. ILO (1993), *Child Labour in Indonesia*, Geneva, ILO, p. 6.
56. ICLSIT (1995), *Child Labour in India : A Perspective*, New Delhi, Govt. of India, pp. 17-18.
57. Morice, A (1981), *op. cit.*, p. 145.
58. *Ibid.*

3. DYNAMICS OF CHILD LABOUR

INFORMAL SECTOR: CHILD LABOUR BASTION

1. *Introduction*

Dualist approach recognized two-sector economy. Earlier dualists used to divide economy between traditional sector and modern sector or industrial and, agricultural sector. However, dualist thinking as Bromley[1] pointed out, got institutionalized with Hart's paper[2] on urban employment in Ghana, which classified economy into formal and informal sectors. The classification came in vogue and established with the *ILO's Employment Mission to Kenya* in 1972. This latest classification is also not free of controversies as reflected by various definitions. It has been defined in various manners such as "all small-scale activity that has little capital and a relatively large labour force and is organized in a non-capitalist way"[3]. However, two types of definitions have emerged from the existing literature. These are: *(i)* functional, and *(ii)* those which are based on characteristics of informal sector. The functional definition runs as "a place where unemployed persons look for job and skills"[4]. Whereas, the other "describes the sector by its attributed characteristics"[5]. None of the definition has been accepted without criticism and reservation. Instead, characteristics have been taken for 'recognizing' and describing the concept of informal sector.

2. *Characteristics of the "Informal Sector"*

The ILO in its report has described the following characteristics of the informal sector.[6]

(*i*) It is easy to enter the informal sector as compared to formal sector in an economy as restrictions e.g. legal, licensing etc. in the informal sector are almost non-existent. However, the informal sector has its own requirements, as far as entry is concerned, thereby placing certain limitations, such as, minimal amount of skills and capital. In certain activities pertaining to household there are no requirements. But other activities such as, marginal manufacturing activities not only skills but also capital is required. Since units operating in the informal sector are so large in number that these have to face intensive competition among themselves as well as with those of the formal sector. Thus, skill requirements have become very high for the survival.

Secondly, finance in the informal sector is mainly from personal and family resources. It is presumed that the requirement of finance is very low in the informal sector and hence it is met from personal and family resources. The reason for low finance is low volume or a small- scale of production.

Thirdly, low starting capital is required in the informal sector since it largely depends on labour-intensive techniques and skills. However, high level of capital borrowing takes place with in the sector and thus it gives the false impression that the capital required to enter the sector is low[7].

Fourthly, informal sector has been characterized by the use of labour intensive techniques. Most of the units in this sector use more component of labour than capital. It is however, alleged that researchers have exaggerated this aspect so as to prove their expectations about employment creation in the informal sector.

Fifthly, informal sector relies on the non-formal system such as apprenticeship and on the job training. All artisans in the handicraft sector have, for example, apprentices and provide on-the- job- training. Similarly, workshops are also known for it.

Bromley[8] has given the following set of characteristics of the informal sector based upon the Kenya[9] report:

(*a*) ease of entry;
(*b*) reliance on indigenous resources;
(*c*) family ownership of enterprises;
(*d*) small-scale of operations;

(*e*) labour-intensive and adopted technology;
(*f*) skills acquired outside the formal school system; and
(*g*) unregulated and competitive markets.

The characteristics given at (*c*), (*d*) and (*g*) need some elaboration since others have been explained in the preceding discussion. Informal sector mainly comprises of family enterprises as a means of self-employment. It naturally has a small-scale operation from which low production is deduced. Another distinct characteristic of the informal sector is that the sector is often regulated and discouraged by the government. It is free from the formalities such as registration, licensing, inspection laws etc. since most of the units come under the category of family enterprises.

The informal sector is highly competitive mainly due to large number of operators producing or selling similar range of goods. These have intensive competition within the sector as well with the established enterprises of the formal sector for their survival and success.

3. *The Concept of the Informal Sector*

What is, then, the concept of the informal sector? Is it traditional or modern? Rural or urban or both? The existing literature has created more confusion than clarification, in particular about its locational aspects. It all started with urbanization as reflected first in Hart's paper than ILO's report cited elsewhere in the chapter. Even members of JASPA (ILO) Regional Employment Team have given impression in their writing that the informal sector is largely an urban phenomenon and it came into existence mainly as a consequence of the rural-urban migration of skilled persons.[10]

There is no doubt that the informal sector is a combination of traditional and modern sectors since the activities carried out in the sector are partly traditional and partly modern characterized by its mode of production. In the nascent stage, informal sector spring up due to migration from rural areas to urban centres hence combining traditional wisdom for urbanized production. The migrants from rural side enter urban activities not requiring high level of skill, even no skills. It was urban production structure which compelled them to learn while earn, i.e. acquire skills to produce new items and services. Hence, it was considered urban phenomenon as it stemmed from the urbanization process. It remained like that through out its early stages. However, similar enterprises later on developed in rural areas. Had it not been the case, there could be no complaint about ignoring the rural informal sector.[11] It may be due to reasons, e.g. (*i*) informal sector came into being due to urbanization processes, (*ii*) it is largely confined to the urban centres and (*iii*) large employment has been provided in the urban informal sector. Hence, the informal sector became synonym of urban area.

It all started with migration of skilled labour, artisans and unskilled job seekers from rural to urban areas. Moreover, many of those who could not get absorbed in the formal sector took refuge under the guise of 'self-employed' and established their family-enterprise. It is true for urbanites as well persons from the rural area. All did not succeed due to intensive competition, poor marketing strategy and lack of finance. Just to name a few factors with the passage of time intense competition, marginal profitability and lack of marketing facilities frustrated some of the workers who have acquired skills and know-how moved towards less green pastures, that is, rural centres and established their 'family- enterprise' in the rural setting. This kind of 'reversal' led to the creation of the rural informal sector and now it deserves as "much attention as the urban informal sector".[12]

Another approach[13] to clarify the concept of the informal sector is breaking it down as per the objectives and means of entrepreneur operating there. There are three categories:

(*i*) informal sector as a traditional activity resulting from the rural urban migration of artisans, (*ii*) the informal sector as an urban activity consequent of modern sector's failure to provide employment and skills and (*iii*) the informal sector as urban small-scale enterprises. Now, is the turn of delineating objectives of each 'type' of sector and its means of attaining objectives. Let it be clear that these are not three informal sectors but only breakdown of the informal sector as per the activities of operators therein.

The segment of the informal sector resulted from the rural-urban migration of artisans has three objectives *viz.* self consumption, subsistence and possible improvement in living standard. Its means are: traditional skills, family labour and capital, social organization.

The other segment of the informal sector characterized by urban activity and providing employment and skills which formal sector failed to provide has the objectives of "alternative to skill acquisition, subsistence/survival, profit and accumulation by the means of skills, family labour and capital, social organization and market information.

The segment of the informal sector characterized by small-scale urban enterprises has three main objectives. These are: managing own business, accumulating capital and profit, avoiding taxes, competition in providing similar goods. To achieve its objectives, means are: adopting skills from the formal sector, taking advantage of market opportunities, saving in banks and obtaining indirect assistance from the formal sector and using family capital and family labour.

What is highlighted by this breakdown of the informal sector? It, in fact, explains that the entry in this sector is for survival of migrants from the rural area and possible improvement in their living standard. And those skilled workers coming from the formal sector to establish their own enterprise aim at profit and capital accumulation. Only this segment uses facilities of banks and financial institutions, that too, very limited. However, the common aspect of all segments of the informal sector is utilization of family labour and capital.

However, aforementioned characteristics and breakdown of the informal sector have overlooked some important features. All the activities in the informal sector revolve mainly around self-employment. It would not be any exaggeration that the informal sector has resulted from the self-employment activities and growth in the sector provided employment opportunities to migrated, artisans, educated-unemployed, and semi-skilled labour. The economies of south Asia, where unemployment is rampant and a large force of educated unemployed exists, is a testimony to this fact.

Another significant but somewhat ignored factor is that there is a very large number of units in the informal sector which is wide-spread. It provides explanation to the characteristics of unregulated nature of the sector and, intensive competition with in the sector. The units are so widely scattered and located even in the houses that their regulation by the government and law enforcing agencies becomes a distant reality.

Similarly, employment pattern in the informal sector 'units' is strikingly different from that of the formal sector. Each of the units provides employment in small number mixed with family members and apprentices. Large number of apprentices with nominal payment and often without payment forms a sizable labour force. However, small number of employed persons other than family members makes majority of units a sort of household activity and thus escaping from various legal formalities and labour laws.

These features, especially self-employment should be given proper placement for the description and analysis of the informal sector, as the self-employment feature is like back-bone of the informal sector in any developing country. For example, informal sector firms are mostly one-man firms in Africa, heavily relying on apprentices[14].

How and why child labour fits in the informal sector? Let us begin with the basic features of the informal sector vis-à-vis child labour.

(*i*) Family Child Labour: Since the informal sector has a dominant role for family labour, it involves family child labour in its economic activities. Certain family skills in handicraft segment of the informal sector are known for engaging their children as skills are passed on from one generation to another. In this tradition children become the link. In many developing countries sequine, needle work, papier-mache, wood and metal crafts are those economic activities in which family child labour is largely employed.

'Self-employed' firms characterized by single owner heavily rely on family child labour. Similarly, agro-based activities in this category largely depend on the contribution of their children. Hence, self-employment which is a striking feature of the informal sector promotes child labour in the sector basically to keep its cost low, a necessity for the survival or subsistence. Thus, family ownership involves directly or indirectly, family child labour in the family enterprise.

Another feature of the informal sector namely, small-scale operation or low-production demands child labour which is cheap and ensures low cost of production which is in turn, necessary for subsistence and survival. It is generally believed that small-scale operations entail relatively high cost of production as compared with large-scale operations in the formal sector. Hence, cheap, that is, child labour becomes the most important factor in determination of the cost level. Why is it that small-scale operations have a relatively high cost of production? The most significant factor responsible for this phenomenon is the scale-economies which are absent in small-scale operations. There are neither external nor internal economies of scale which lead to relatively high cost of production. The family ownership and small-scale operation also necessitates apprentices with nominal or no payment. Almost all the workshops related with wood or metal work and automobile service centres employ apprentices. These are generally young children, as young as six/seven years of age. Child labour in the form of trainees or apprentices is a common feature where the employer's objective is to minimize the cost of production or operation.

Labour-intensive production is another significant feature of the informal sector. It is no exaggeration that bulk of the cost of production in the informal sector is constituted of labour. The range of labour content in total cost may vary between two-third and three-fourth. If the going wage rate is paid and adult workers are employed, venture may become too costly leading to its closure. Hence, to minimize the cost of production child labour as wage earner at a low wage-rate and children as apprentices, with some nominal or without payment, are employed. Labour-intensive method of production makes it easy and possible to employ child labour since skills can be easily acquired by children. Therefore, the nature of production method and the high labour cost input paves the way for child labour in such a sector.

Since skill acquisition in the labour-intensive informal sector where a minimum professional or technical qualification is necessary, children get entry as trainees, apprentices or manual workers to run errands in the unit. This is true not only in the case of small-scale units but in agricultural sector as well. The development of capitalist agriculture in Ghana during the late 60s provides an example where "as the rice industry boomed, young men, some scarcely in their teens, flocked to attach themselves as apprentices or mates to tractor drivers employed by private farmers or state companies. This influx, coupled with unemployment as farmers reduced their acreage after three years of drought, enabled farmers to increase the already rampant exploitation of tractor drivers and their mates...Faced with unemployment, however, young workers were prepared to accept these poor conditions just to keep their jobs; the status of 'apprentice', such that it was, disappeared as young workers remained mates for 5, 6 or 7 years"[15] Hence, the method of imparting training to young children for acquisition of skills in an informal system, or outside the formal school system, leads to employment and exploitation of children.

The 'unregulated and competitive markets' characteristic of the informal sector largely supports and even encourages, the employment of child labour. Since activities in the informal sector including its units are wide-spread hence difficult to be regulated by the inspection system generally prevailing in developing countries. Secondly, most of the units in the informal sector are family enterprises employing less than ten, do not fall under the purview of labour or child labour laws. They take advantage of either loop-holes in the legal provisions and system or inspectorate, i.e. administrative system, or both. Therefore, child labour as contravention to child labour laws gets ample opportunity of employment though at a lower wage or as 'apprentices' without difficulty.

Since the number of units operating in the informal sector is large even in one-line of production, intensive competition is a natural outcome. Hence, the product commands a low price. There is, moreover, competition not only with in the sector but also between the sectors. It is further, deterrent to high level of prices for the products of informal sector. Again, price has to be kept low. Keeping in view the labour 'input' in the production, employers are bound to employ cheap labour in order to be competitive in the market. Hence, demand for child labour which has plentiful supply at a low wage-rate. The unregulated nature and competitiveness creates large demand for child labour in the informal sector of any developing country.

To sum-up the demand for child labour in the informal sector, determinants of demand may be delineated as: (low) wage-rate, family ownership of enterprises, reliance on labour-intensive technology, nature of skills, i.e. skills not requiring any formal or institutionalized training, unregulated and highly competitive markets. However, cheap wage-rate is the main determinant of demand for child labour while the rest of the factors may be described as 'derived' determinants- making child employment atmosphere conducive.

MODES OF PRODUCTION AND CHILD LABOUR

The structure and requirements of the informal sector give rise to child labour. It, however, can not explain *in toto* the system which originates total demand for child labour in an economy. Something else has to be taken into account which may shed more light on the creation of niches for child labour. It is the mode of production and its transitions in a society which may explain what a discussion on the informal sector vis-à-vis child labour could not describe. "The concept of the mode of production highlights the fact that it is not just the nature of the work or the setting in which it occurs that is important, but also the social organization of work and the factors that determine this organization, be they ecological, economic, political or cultural."[16] Therefore, merely a description of setting and nature of activities therein fall short of explanation necessary to discuss child labour and its related aspects.

Modes of production may broadly be divided into two

categories. These are : (*i*) pre-capitalist and (*ii*) capitalist mode of production, that is, transition to industrial capitalism.

1. *Pre-capitalist Mode of Production and Child Labour*

In the pre-capitalist society characterized by primitive technology, such as, pastoral, nomadic or hunting and gathering, division of labour from social point of view was limited in the sense that everyone contributed as per one's capability for survival. The tasks performed by age, sex or capacity in such a society could be divided into : (*i*) effort-intensive and (*ii*) time-intensive where the former had usually been ascribed to adults in their prime age, while the latter to the mostly young children[17]. Children, for example, in an agrarian society have been employed for mending cattles, assisting in weeding, sowing and harvesting. These were time-intensive activities generally assigned to young children. Still in rural areas, child labour is being utilized for time-intensive task and adult workers generally do effort- intensive work. In other words, adult effort-intensive work gets facilitated by time-intensive tasks performed by children. In such a social division of labour based on age, gender and capacity, the amount of work is very limited. However, in such a mode of production, e.g. lineage mode of production prevalent in Africa, a surplus is received from the direct producers which in turn, explains exploitation of child labour. Similarly, in a peasant family production system, children are integrated into various adult task, albeit gradually and thus children assume the role of producers. Children of Kith and Kin are also integrated either for household work or employed as producer of labour power for production activities and hence get exploited at an early age.

A pre-capitalist such as feudal society leads to intensive work and thereby more exploitation of child labour. In a typical feudal system, whole family is supposed to provide labour services to the landlord as socio-economic, religious and political obligations. Children along with their parents have to contribute for surplus production and hence appropriation of their surplus labour takes place. It is the child labour which is, in such circumstances, more exploited. In such a social environment, child labour is employed and intensive work leads to growing exploitation as being producer and also in terms of socialization function of schooling which is foregone. A peasant family due to its rental obligation integrated child labour into adult work, thus resulting in exploitation.

In feudal class relations, the most important instrument used to employ children and exploit them is debt bondage. Some specific features of the system encourage the use of child labour. These are [18]:

(*a*) for a paltry sum of money as a loan or advance, child of the family is mortgaged. This kind of debt bondage is very common in a number of developing countries. The child, in return, has to work with partial payment or without payment, till the amount along with interest is repaid. However, it rarely happens as the interest rate charged is generally exorbitant. It leads to further exploitation of child labour;

(*b*) Sometimes loanee sends child for the compulsory services as own's substitute. Such practice is common in rural areas. It depends upon the terms and conditions of loan when it is agreed upon that the loanee shall do certain service compulsorily till the loan is repaid. For example, milching of cattle etc. then the loanee may get his/her son engaged for such services. Hence, the child works as substitute for the parent. This practice also encourages child labour especially in rural area and in the household sector.

(*c*) There is, sometimes agreement or understanding that the dependent of bonded person shall be doing work along with the bonded person. The feudal system in India and Pakistan encouraged child labour and exploited children through the system known as *begar*. In Indian context Dube's[19] study exposes the use of child labour and its exploitation under various systems prevailing which are feudal in nature. Though feudal relations and the use of child labour vary from place to place, debt is the most common factor encouraging the use of child labour in most developing countries ridden with feudal or semi-feudal relations of production.

2. *Industrial Capitalism*

The growth of industrial capitalism may be characterized by increase in industrial production, rise of cash crops, skill oriented labour market and wage employment etc. All the countries have not developed in the same manner but these have some common characteristics. However, development in the country led to growing importance of schooling, education, training and on-the-job training etc. These factor have besides skill requirement and technology adoption, adversely affected the employment of children. Hence, there was a long-term decline in the employment of child labour in such a system.

In most of the countries, large firms and industries or other establishments, commonly known as the formal sector, has no place for child labour. Its main reasons are skill requirement, demand for trained and technical labour force and laws against the use of child labour. The formal sector adopted such technology and developed capitalist relation of production which made the child labour redundant in this sector.

However, the process of capital and profit accumulation in the informal sector resulted largely as a consequence of the failure of the formal sector to absorb growing labour force, skilled and unskilled both, created demand for cheap labour, that is, child labour. Children working alongside parents sell their labour to earn 'supplementary' wage. It fits well in the capital and profit accumulation system of the informal sector, thus leading to ever-growing employment and use of child labour and exploitation.

The capitalist relations of production turned out as substitute for feudal and semi-feudal production relations. The wage employment, an essential characteristic of capitalist relations of production, paved the way for itself in the rural sector. This has encouraged the children of subsistence or peasant farmers to look for outward wage employment. Moreover, growing landlessness in the rural sector has also contributed to the growth of capitalist relations by means of wage employment.

The division of labour, another inherent factor of capitalist relations, got modified and favoured child labour for labour-intensive production in the informal sector where formal training and education, a pre-requisite in the formal sector, is not required. Thus the scope for child labour in the informal sector has increased. Moreover, the unregulated nature of the informal sector has especially encouraged the use of child labour.

To sum-up, the capitalist relations of production *per se* do not favour the use of child labour since its bias towards formal sector which, in turn, has no place for employment of children due to technological, social such as unionization and legal reasons. But a transition to industrial capitalism has also developed a parallel sector, that is, informal sector. This sector has such modes of production which create niche for the use of child labour. Hence, it raised the demand for child labour.

REFERENCES

1. Bromley, R (1978), "Introduction- The urban informal sector : Why is it Worth Discussing"?, *World Development,* pp. 1033-39.
2. Hart, K (1973), "Informal Income Opportunities and Urban Employment in Ghana", *Journal of Modern African Studies,* March issue.
3. Morice, A (1981), "The Exploitation of Children in the 'Informal Sector': Proposals for Research", in G. Rodgers & G. Standing (eds.), *Child Work, Poverty and Underdevelopment,* Geneva, ILO, p. 137.
4. Aboagye, A.A. & K.M. Gozo (1986), "The Informal Sector: A Critical Appraisal of the Concept", in JASPA (ed). *The Challenge of Employment & Basic Needs in Africa,* Nairobi, Oxford University Press, p. 265.
5. *Ibid.*
6. *Ibid*, pp. 263-64.
7. *Ibid*, p. 263.
8. Bromley, R. (1995), "The Urban Informal Sector", in J. Ennew (ed), *Learning or Labouring?,* Florence, UNICEF, p. 10.
9. ILO (1972), *Employment, Incomes and Equity: A Strategy for Increasing Productive Employment in Keyna,* Geneva, ILO.
10. Aboagye, A.A. & K.M. Gozo (1986), *op. cit.,* p. 264.
11. Bromley, R (1995), *op. cit,* p. 10.
12. *Ibid.*
13. Aboagye, A.A. & K.M. Gozo (1986), *op.cit.,* pp. 264-65.
14. JASPA (1986), "The Informal Sector in Africa", in JASPA (ed.), *The Challenge of Employment & Basic Needs in Africa,* Nairobi, Oxford University Press, p. 259.
15. Van Hear, N. (1995), "Child Labour and the Development of Capitalist

Agriculture in Ghana", in Judith Ennew (ed.), *op. cit.,* p. 62.

16. Schildkrout, E. (1981), "The Employment of Children in Kano (Nigeria)", in G. Rodgers & G. Standing (eds.), *Child Work, Poverty and Under Development,* Geneva, ILO, p. 99.
17. Rodgers, G. & G. Standing (1981), "The Economic Roles of Children : Issues for Analysis", in G. Rodgers & G. Standing (eds.), *op. cit.,* p. 13.
18. Dube, L. (1981), "The Economic Roles of Children in India: Methodological Issues", G. Rodgers & G. Standing (eds.), *op. cit.,* p. 198.
19. *Ibid.,* pp. 179-213.

4. WHERE ARE CHILDREN EMPLOYED?

Child Labour is all pervasive in the sense that it is employed in the organized and unorganized sectors of the economy in one way or the other, particularly in developing countries. Although the use of child labour varies from place to place and activity to activity. Some sectors are infamous for the use and exploitation of child labour. Is it possible to identify those niches where child labour is overwhelmingly employed? Various empirical studies have helped in such identification and now child labour has been classified under four heads. These are[1]: (*i*) industry and construction, (*ii*) service trades, (*iii*) domestic service, and (*iv*) agriculture. Though the classification does not conform any standardized form, such as, traditional-modern sector, formal-informal sector, agricultural-industrial sector etc., yet it highlights the concentration of child labour. By activity, child labour in developing countries is largely used in agriculture, handicrafts, marginal economic activities like petty trading and services and small-scale industries forming the backbone of the informal sector.

1. AGRICULTURE

The largest number of child worker has been engaged in the agricultural sector due to traditional, cultural and socio-economic factors. It has been a tradition in agrarian society to use child labour. Subsistence agriculture has always depended upon child labour due to socio-economic reasons. It can not afford to hire wage labour as it has small holdings where surplus is nominal or non-existent. However, a distinction should be made between working on the own land and working for other's land as hired labour. In traditional societies, children work on their own lands alongwith other family members. In such cases there is no question of remuneration, hence child labour is unpaid. It does not amount to exploitation as working conditions are neither harsh nor discriminatory. The parents engaging their young children assign them light works which are usually time-intensive and not effort intensive. They care for their working children. Subsistence farmers take the assistance of their children during sowing and harvesting periods when the agricultural operations are time-bound and hired labour is beyond their means. Similarly, farming on share-cropping basis also encourages the use of child labour due to the same reason.

On the contrary, child labour used for commercial agriculture is always subjected to exploitation in terms of remuneration, time and work. Child labourer is invariably hired to work in the field as it commands low wage and works for longer hours. Since the supply of child labour is plentiful, it has no organization to protect or to safeguard its interest e.g. trade union and sells itself in a 'buyers' market, child labour becomes vulnerable as commercium and hence exploited. The capitalist relations of production in commercial agriculture gave rise to wage-employment of working children. This is agriculture as 'enterprise' which attracts child labour and employs as hired labour on wage-basis. It is, however, noticed that the nature of employment for child labour is either casual or *ad-hoc* or a mix of the two. Children are hired daily or seasonally for a particular period, i.e., sowing and or harvesting season but at a fixed wage-rate. The nature of work is both time-intensive and effort-intensive. The capitalist mode of production aiming at profit accumulation has inherent characteristic of exploitation and in the absence of safeguarding organization, e.g., union, children are intensively exploited by their employers.

The best illustration of capitalistic agricultural development causing demand for child labour is that of Ghana's paddy cultivation in the late 60s[2]. The highly commercial nature of paddy cultivation resulted in migration of labour from the cocoa area of the North to the food farms. When the rice farming took off in the Dagomba district itself, it increased the demand for hired labour in the area. Farmers looking for cheap labour encouraged the use of child labour and were termed as 'allaha', i.e. wanting cheap.[3] Children as casual labourers then formed the bulk of labour force working on rice farms due to cheap wages and long working hours. The farmers exploited child labour not only by paying low wage-rate and sometimes refused to pay or attempted to delay payment but also argued about the quantum of work which led to the eruption of violence by young working children[4]. However, children employed in rice industry on wage- employment as never before also induced the use of child labour in other occupations such as rice milling, marketing and, in the construction[5].

Wherever semi-feudal or feudal society exists, child labour is exploited on account of traditions or customs. Landlords usually exploit labour including child labour by asking them to work in their field without any payment. Such a system is also prevailing in some areas in India where they have to work on lands belonging to the temple without any remuneration.

The feudal system has encouraged forced labour in a significant manner. The term forced labour means "all work or service which is exacted from any person under the menace of any penalty and for which the said person has not offered himself voluntarily"[6]. In India, for example, caste system is deep-rooted in the society and it is also reflected in agrarian system. Bihar one of the poorest and caste-ridden province in India, still has a semi-feudal agricultural system in its backward regions. Here the high caste rich farmers and landlords force the landless poor labourers of the low caste to work on their land. Children along with family are thus coerced and results in forced labour. It is being a practice in the name of the caste system where forced labour is either not paid or a low wage-rate is forced upon the landless and poor agricultural workers belonging to a low caste. Any resistance leads to suppression and eruption of violence in the villages. The forced labour is coerced and never voluntarily, it is invariably under-paid, particularly in the case of child labour.

The commercial agriculture and plantation have largely contributed in the exploitation of child labour by means of bonded labour. It would be better to distinguish between forced' and 'bonded' labour where the latter always implies the former but vice-versa may not be invariably true. The U.N. has defined debt bondage (bonded labour) as "the status or conditions arising from a pledge by a debtor of his personal services or of those of a person under his control as security for a debt. If the value of those services as reasonably assessed is not applied towards the liquidation of debt or the length and nature of those services are not respectively limited and defined"[7]. And the person under control is a child whose services are pledged[8]. The term bonded labour refers to "the master-labour relationship, the principal feature of which is the pledging of children against a loan or an agreement between the child and the employer whereby the child would work throughout its life in exchange for money or food"[9].

A child becomes bonded labour when pledged for some money advance or credit and labour is pledged for an indefinite period of time. In this process child is traded like a commodity as parents have absolute power over their children[10]. It is irony that bonded labourers can terminate bondage by paying off their debt but rarely it happens due to low wages and usurious interest rate. Debt sometimes increases despite servitude when the employer charges for tools, food or accommodation, and will often levy fines for unsatisfactory work[11]. In such a situation debt can never be repaid and passes on from one generation to the next generation.[12].

Bonded labour is widely prevalent in South Asia and Latin America. It is known by different names in different countries, such as, *peshgi gehna makhlooq* in Pakistan and *enganche* in Peru[13] and their number is very large. In the case of India, number as noted by the ILO runs in several millions only in the agricultural sector.[14] Other countries having bonded child labourer are Brazil, Dominican Republic and some more from Latin America.

The extent of the use of child labour in agriculture may be judged from "that a majority of all work done by children is in agriculture".[15] There is, perhaps, no developing country where the rise and exploitation of child labour is not prevalent. Children as unpaid family helpers in subsistence farming can be found in Lesotho, Botswana, Burundi, Kenya, Ethiopia—all over Africa since child labour has been accepted as an integral part of the economic and social pattern of life.[16]

Child Labour in Commercial Agriculture

African continent known for its harsh geography has commercial agriculture not in any significant manner. Agriculture here is confined to either communal or family farming for own and local consumption of few crops grown on these farms. However, plantations are found along the coastal countries of West Africa and the countries of East African Plateau, that is, from the Ethiopian high lands to South Africa producing coffee, cocoa, tea, cotton, rice, rubber, vanilla and sisal. While vegetable and fruits are largely grown in South Africa.

Agriculture including plantation usually hires child labour on contract basis while the working conditions for child labour are very harsh. "Climatic conditions quickly induce fatigue; there is a constant danger from insects, reptiles and other animals, the ground is hard and tools primitive; distances to be travelled are sometimes very great; working hours are long; and the overall picture can be even worse if the children themselves are not in good health."[17]

Child labour is generally hired through some middlemen. Farmers may have contract with tribal chiefs in the region and children, on contract, are hired. During the harvest season even school children are either hired or compelled to work on the farms particularly government farms. Owners of commercial farms, for example, in Tanazania hired as young as six years of age for plantation work[18], whereas school children in Chipinge and Chisumbange in Zimbabwe were force to pick up cotton during harvesting season in November 1990 with a threat that refusal shall result in their expulsion.[19]

There seems the use of child labour on a large-scale on farms growing vegetables, grapes for wine, maize, sugarcane and tobacco in South Africa. ILO estimated that more than 60,000 young children between 8 and 14 years worked on these farms in 1987 and government inspectors were not allowed, till 1994, to inspect any private commercial farms in South Africa.[20]

Young children alongwith their mothers pick coffee berries in Kenya while older children work independently. The demand for children on coffee plantation goes up during the harvesting season and is estimated around 58 percent of total workforce on coffee plantations in Kenya; while it remains 18 per cent through out the year. [21] The working children earn so less and work for long hours which adversely affect their health[22]. Similarly, children work on coffee plantations in Madagascar, Uganda, Cote d' Ivoire and other countries growing and exporting coffee.

Child labour for picking cotton is used *in toto* since wages are so low that no adult worker, even unemployed do not accept in Zimbabwe. Besides children, only migrant labour families do work whereby children are also involved due to piece rate payment. The use of child labour is growing, though it is a work traditionally performed by women in Zimbabwe.

Analogously, tea estates in Zimbabwe hire children as young as 10 to 12 years and part-time or contract work is offered. The school going children work and if their minimum daily load is less they are forced to work on week end. Moreover the usual work hazards such as abdominal pain and cuts in the hands and legs from tea bushes are common[23]. Similarly, children are also employed on tobacco plantations in Zimbabwe and South Africa. They spread pesticides with bare hands and working conditions are harsh while wage is meagre.

Sisal plantations in Tanzania usually hire children to cultivate, transplant and weed throughout the year, while it is hazardous work since it causes lung disease. The workforce in sisal industry consists as large proportion of young children as 30 per cent and migrant children sometimes also work for their friends and relatives.[24].

Asian subcontinent, particularly India is having the largest number of working children in the World and child labour is overwhelmingly concentrated in the agricultural sector. These children work on farms and plantations. In Pakistan, for example, it is estimated that there are three million children working in the agricultural sector.[25] Bangladesh also has a large proportion i.e. 82 percent of its active population of children in agricultural sector.[26]

Another country in Asia having a large child labour force in its agricultural sector in Indonesia where more than 82 percent of boys and 64 percent of girls of the age group 10 to 14 years are engaged in agricultural activities like palm, rubber, tea and tobacco plantations[27]. Similarly, in Thailand around 85 percent of the child workforce is in the agricultural sector.[28] All these statistics point towards large employment of children in the agricultural sector of Asian countries, such as, India, Pakistan, Bangladesh, Nepal, Srilanka, Malaysia, Indonesia and Philippines etc. However, plantations have a large employment of child workers on hired or contract basis. Indian tea estates, particularly in Assam and West Bengal employ children somewhere between 21000 and 77000 [29], though this demand for child labour is highly seasonal and attract migrant workers.

Vegetable farms in the Philippines have a large number of child workers to weed, cultivate, and harvest the crop for a meagre daily payment of 25 pesos, i.e. half of the wage of an adult worker. A case study[30] of vegetable farms in the Benguet province highlights the harsh working conditions for child labour and falling victim to health hazards.[31]

Child labour in Malaysia[32] is used on palm and rubber plantations. However, most of the children work as part of a family unit. There is restriction to tap atleast a fixed number of trees only then the worker would be entitled for his daily wage. Hence, children are also engaged by their parents to assist them and they perform many supporting tasks.[33]

In Thailand children are recruited through some agents and debt bondage is a practice to hire children for sugarcane plantations.[34] The exploitation of child labour in Thailand is not confined to agriculture or plantations but also in fishing, an allied sector of agriculture. In the case of fishing, very young children under 14 years are engaged and involved in all stages of the fishing business. Here migrant workers outnumber resident workers. For meagre salaries ranging between $ 22 to $ 69 a month, they are employed for cleaning and sorting etc. Their work hours are very long and lack of protective facilities like gloves etc. force them to take off two or three days every month because of hand problems.[35]

Child labour exploitation is most in deep sea fishing. There is a significant number of children working in this sector in the Philippines[36] where training begins at a young age as diver. Young children working for *Muro-ami* fishing perform hazardous task of diving deep into the sea and stay there till net is hauled in the boat. They also have to stay at sea for three to four weeks at a stretch without proper sanitation and other facilities. Though it may be an under estimation, Marine Fishery Census found around two and a half thousand children aged between 11 and 14 years employed in this hazardous[37] task.

Indonesia has more harsh working condition for children. They are employed on offshore fishing platforms numbering between 700 and 1500, particularly in Northern Sumatra, as forced labour. Each platform employs three to ten young children between 10 and 18 years, recruited by unscrupulous agents[38]. Similarly, bonded child labour has been used in Srilanka, particularly on small islands of the north western and eastern coasts, although it is assumed to have been eliminated as militants more probably destroyed such fishing camps.[39] However, the use of child labour on plantations in Sri Lanka is quite prominent.

Indian fishing sector has an estimated 20,000 strong child labour force only in Kerala. A number of children working in this sector come under the category of bonded labour and are severely exploited.[40] There are a number of states like Kerala, Tamilnadu, Maharashtra and Andhra Pradesh, Bengal and Orissa where child labour is used in the fishing sector. Mostly agents recruit these children by paying some advance money to the parents and hence children become bonded labour, subject to severe exploitation[41]. Labour in bondage takes worst form when entire families are entrapped and exploited as the cases from Pakistan have been reported[42].

The facts and figure presented here help in classifying child labour used in agricultural and allied sectors. Child labour, on the basis of remuneration and or working condition may be divided in to : (*i*) wage employment, (*ii*) Contract employment (Seasonal) both the categories come under supplementary wages, (*iii*) forced labour, and (*iv*) bonded labour where wages are either nil or nominal and working conditions are harsh as compared with that of the first two categories.

Another region known for the use of child labour in agriculture is Latin America where prominent countries in this regard are Mexico, Central American countries, the Andean Countries, Argentina and Brazil.

The plantation sector in Gautemala attracts every year around 300,000 labourers from the highland to work on coffee, sugarcane, cardamom and cotton plantations, while 27 to 32 percent of these migrant labour are young children between the ages of 12 and 14 years and paid only half of adult worker's payment[43]. Brazil has three million strong child labours force in its rural areas working on tea, tobacco, sugarcane and sisal plantations; and most of the child labour in agriculture in northeastern states which are poor but, at the same time, rich states as Sao Paulo, Minas Gerais and Parana etc. also employ child labour for agricultural activities.[44] In Brazil, increasing mechanization of agriculture and plantation forced out labourers and their family earnings were reduced substantially which, in turn, compelled them to press their children as *'boias-frias'* (meaning cold food, which is carried by them) and *'volantes'* (meaning in movement to refer labour hired for one season and which moves to other place for new contract). In the same manner, child labour has been a tradition in the rural areas of the Andean Region's countries, e.g. Ecuador where children work on farms and Banana plantations to 'supplement' the household income. Illegal immigrants from Bolivia and Paraguay, and their children work on tobacco, tea and soy plantations in Argentina. Peru's agriculture is no exception where the use of child labour is quite large scale, i.e. around 7.5 million children under 15 years of age are employed.[45] It is estimated that atleast 70 percent of total child labour is employed in the agricultural sector of Peru. Similarly, 45 percent of total child labour works in agricultural sector of Mexico and they are between 12 and 15 years of age.

Children along with women have replaced permanent adult workers on plantations since they are paid lower wage-rate and hence child labour, in some cases, has increased[46]. Children as young as 6 years old are engaged on coffee plantations in Honduras and they constitute approximately 20 per cent of the labour force during planting and harvesting seasons. However these children work along with their parents on piece-rate basis and paid equal to the adult worker's wage. However, the use of child labour, particularly for melon and watermelon has been on an increase in Honduras. This is estimated to be up by 25 percent.

In the Latin American countries, child labour is hired through agents, such as '*gatos*' in Brazil on contract basis. They work along with their parents. The number of working children in agriculture including plantations is very large in Brazil, Mexico and Peru. Generally wage-rate is low for children and they work for long-hours. In some countries bonded child labour is also found. It is possible since child labourers are not registered with plantations and farms and hence, have no official status. In this region, migrant labour is an important feature that engage their children along with them in agriculture and plantation work. However, working conditions are tantamount to the exploitation of very young children.[47]

Child labour is not only persisting in developing countries of Asia, Africa and Latin America but also on the rise. It has been in employment maximally in the agricultural sector including plantations and fishing. The common features are : (*i*) children are employed and exploited at a very young age in terms of wages, working hours and other working conditions, (*ii*) their employment is illegal and hence has no official status, (*iii*) they are bonded through advance amounts and recruited by agents, besides contract employment, (*iv*) the nature of their employment is temporary, (*v*) demand for child labour increases substantially during sowing/planting and harvesting seasons, (*vi*) piece-rate payment is common as it exploits to the maximum, (*vii*) child labour laws are most ineffective in the rural areas of these countries that's why demand for and employment of children in agricultural sector has been rising, atleast in certain countries, and (*viii*) more under developed and in the interior a region is, more is the number of working children.

2. INDUSTRY AND CONSTRUCTION

Child labour next to agriculture, is largely used in this sector which includes a large number of activities and marginal manufacturing units including cottage industries or handicrafts, light industries such as textiles and cloth, food processing and canning, confectionery, works like weaving, sewing, embroidery, shoes, toys, buttons, clothing, fire works and workshops, i.e. metal work, woodwork and leather work. The list is long, so are the activities for which child labour is hired.

What are specific reasons encouraging the use of child labour in these segments of an economy? Some of these may be stated as : informal nature of these sectors and activities, formal training is not required, labour-intensive mode of production, unregulated activities, high demand for cheap labour, traditional suitability of child labour to certain works especially handicrafts and, family ownership.

Let us begin with traditional factors occupying an important place in various societies. In many developing countries there is tradition of child labour as an integral process of educating for life. Secondly, assistance of children in the family occupation,. Thirdly, passing on family skills especially in handicrafts is also a tradition among artisans. Fourthly, caste or community based professions, works engage family children as a social custom or tradition.

Another factor largely responsible for the use of child labour in these segments is family ownership of enterprises. These single owner units are the general outcome of self-employment and hence engage their children for assistance as employment of hired labour becomes burden some. In such cases, child labour is unpaid and motivating factor is authority or absolute power[48] of parents over their children.

The system of on-the-job training and apprenticeship without remuneration or bare minimum payment also creates space for children in metal work, wood work, leather work and small manufacturing units. Children gain experience and skills while employer gets helping hands without incurring expenditure. Child labour in such a system is exploited for many years and employers minimize their cost of production necessary for their survival or competition.

Certain crafts are considered suitable for children. Hand-knotted carpet manufacturing is one of them. India, Pakistan, Nepal, Iran, Egypt and Morocco employed only children for the weaving of hand-knotted carpets one or the other time. Similarly, match and *beedi* (local cigarette) making are the other production activities in India, Pakistan and Nepal etc. where children are largely employed. Their physique, temperament and attitude towards these activities are best suited to the profession or this is what the employers think. Gem Polishing in India is usually done by children. This attitude of employers that children are best suited to certain task promotes the use of child labour. Similar jobs are packaging, pasting and labelling, i.e. where a monotonous pace is required, children are particularly useful for the employer.[49]

Construction is another segment where children are employed in Asia, Latin America and even in South Europe. It is common to see children at construction sites doing odd jobs. They are hired as casual labourers and paid less than an adult labourer. A child worker in the construction sector does as much work as an adult labourer with respect to certain tasks. For example, child worker as brick layer's assistant is as efficient as an adult, works for same hours and under same conditions but gets less wage. Migrant families and their children, as may be seen in India and Latin America, get work in the construction industry as entry is simple. Construction sites are rarely without children and women, particularly in south-east Asian countries.

In the construction industry, child workers are generally hired as casual labour on daily wage-rate or on contractual basis. It is usually hired by the sub-contractors on fixed wage-rate for a period. Hence, the involvement of middleman leads to greater exploitation of child labour. It is satisfactory to note that there is at least, no apprenticeship as it is in the light and cottage industries.

3. SERVICE TRADES

Large member of children work in this sector in all developing, and even in some industrial, countries. These can be divided into : (*i*) Children working in establishments such as shops, restaurants and hotels, garages and workshops providing services and (*ii*) Children working on streets selling various types of goods, known as vendors, ranging from newspapers to household items. Infact, number of street children is very large and these are confined to urban centres.

Children working in the service trades is essentially an urban phenomenon. They can be found in every city and town in every developing country without any exception. They are rather there as a rule. There is a complex and overlapping range of variants responsible for this phenomenon. What are socio-economic factors accounting for it? The family in its entirety as a productive survival unit is bound to utilize every member to share responsibilities. Hence, children are invariably involved and work according to their capacity to share the burden. They can not be the bread earner due to their biological and other social limitations, working children simply 'supplement' family income for the sake of survival. Secondly, average income happens to be so low of a family that it presses all its labour potential to use and this drags children in the process of earning. A child-woman-man stratification of income takes the shape similar to the stratification, existing in other sectors. Lack of social or state protection for low income or earning, of the families becomes another factor inducing children for work at an early age. Some developing but industrial countries like India have introduced state protection to what they call 'economically weaker sections' of the society, but its coverage is not sufficient and, low income or earning families are left out. Hence, children work usually in service trades. Cultural factors are also, some times, observed in the case of child labour. In the sub-continent of India, socio-economically backward minorities supply more child labour. In India, muslim minority has a larger proportion of child labour and, that too, in the service trades. Similarly in Peru, children work is associated with *Indian* and *Mestizo* races and not with white Peruvians.[50] Another reason is related with caste system, as in the southeast Asian societies, or racial orientation, which may be observed even in the West, promoting child labour in certain either castes or races. 'Equal opportunity' and other such slogans could not substantially improve the situation. Old customs, traditions, belief and attitude and even racial feelings, though waning, have not disappeared. Children belonging to such strata of social or racial hierarchy could be found working in service trades or household sector.

Social relations do play a role in the employment of working children in the service trades. These are relatives, friends or simple acquaintices which promote child labour in the sector. They cut across the cultural barriers in a developing country. Children belonging to one religious community may be working with the other community's member due to social relations, even in a caste-ridden society, e.g. India, Bangladesh and Pakistan.

In the service trades sector, a vast number of working children, known as street children, exists. They are visible in every city of every developing country. "Street children' is the generic term used to refer to a group of children with a special relationship to the street."[51] These are often divided into *'children on the street'* and *'children of the street'* where the former refers to children who use the street as their work place while the latter means children living on the street. However, the U.N. classification generally used in the country report[52] divided street children into three categories *viz.* (*i*) Children on the street, (*ii*) Children of the street, and (*iii*) Children on and of the street. The first category children use street as their work place during day-time, selling articles like cigarettes, candy, newspapers etc. or providing services such as car washing and watching, shoe-shining, carrying loads etc. They return to their home in the night and hence have family ties and protection of their guardians or parents. The second category, i.e. children of the street refers to those children who not only use streets as their work place but also live on the streets. Such children have no relationships with family and guardians or parents, while the third category refers children who work on streets and spent their nights at home and sometimes on the street. These definitions have raised certain problems as encountered, during the course of research, by Glauser[53]. However, differentiation either as 'children of the street' and 'children on and of the street' both categorization fail to distinguish between children with self-employment, children hired on commission and children engaged by parents/guardians. Such differentiation is necessary as it affects the quality of life and also the degree of exploitation of street children.

Working street children may be classified as per the nature of economic activities. They may be the owner of their selling and servicing activities and hence are 'self-employed'. If the child purchases, say, packets of candy with own money- either earned, saved or borrowed, it is self-employment. Secondly, if the child is contracted or hired as is the case with the newspaper selling, then the working child may be categorized as 'hired or contract labour'. Lastly selling activities may be financed by guardians/ parents where a large proportion of income goes to them, the working child is just a 'residue-retainer' in the sense that he gets what is left to him by his guardian/parents. So, one more classification of street children based on their economic activities, may be added, that is, (*i*) self-employed street children, (*ii*) hired or contract working street children, and (*iii*) 'residue-retainer' working street children. In such a classification, degree of economic exploitation also differs. It is most in the second category, less in the third while the least in the first category. In socio-economic studies such a classification may prove more useful rather than other classifications such as street children (*a*) on the street, (*b*) of the street and (*c*) on and of the street.

Now the economic activities of street children may be classified as: (*i*) selling or street vending, (*ii*) servicing, and (*iii*) clandestine activities—either illegal or immoral. However, distribution of street children may vary from place to place. In Latin American countries, particularly in Brazil, Peru and Mexico where street children problem is extremely severe, they are largely engaged in street vending and then comes servicing such as shoe-shining. A Lima Agriculture University Survey provides following percentage distribution: street vendors 40%, newspaper sellers 6.7%, shoe-shiners 6.7%, car washer 13.5%, barrow boys 8.3%, bus fare collectors 2.2%, artists 5.3%, beggars 3.7% and others 13.5%[54]. It is estimated that there are 30 million working children in Latin America.[55] However, the figure quoted here is not that of street children but of working children in Latin America. Moreover, percentage distribution merely reflects a rough estimate about the distribution of working children, hence, a pattern may only be visualized or assumed for Latin American countries plagued with the problem of street children.

Similar scenario is existing in Asia, particularly south-east Asian countries. The most populated countries in this region like India, Bangladesh, Pakistan and Sri Lanka suffer from a large population of street children. It has become such a gigantic problem that figures have lost their importance.

African continent also faces the ever growing problem of street children. They are engaged in selling, begging, servicing and thieving activities. The reasons for children working on streets are some what different from that of Asia or Latin America. Besides poverty, lack of educational, social protection facilities, and family breakdowns, other factors responsible and which distinguish Africa's problem from other regions is large-scale internal and external displacement of children due to war and ethnic-strife. A large number of countries in Africa are entangled with each other in war or there is ethnic strife and hence, families and particularly children have been displaced in a very large number. In search of safer place they migrate to cities and capital towns. In order to survive in a new environment without any job prospects, they settle for streetism. The recent war between Eritrea and Ethiopia has aggravated the number of street children and their economic activities for survival. The number of street children due to internal displacement has swelled up.

The last category of working street children is that of engaged in clandestine activities such as illegal activities of drug trafficking, theft and largely child sex activities. The last mentioned activity has assumed such a proportion in certain Asian countries like, Thailand and the Philippines that it is sometimes termed as sex-industry where abuse of children is common. India, Bangladesh and Nepal are also facing the problem of sex-services involuntarily provided by minor children. It cuts even across the border. Latin America and Africa are also grappling with this problem.

The U.N. has defined it as "the sexual exploitation of a child for remuneration in cash or kind, usually but not always organized by an intermediary....."[56] The ILO has expressed its concern regarding this form of child labour. It has been estimated that the number may be between 200,000 and 800,000.[57] The most disturbing fact is that there seems to be growing demand for minor children under 15, not only in Asia but also in Latin America.[58] Figures may be controversial but not the subject, i.e., child workers in the sex industry in developing countries. One simple reason put forth is poverty. But other factors have now gained recognition. These are illegal and fraudulent practices of trafficking children for sex work. Tourism has especially promoted child labour in the sex industry of Sri Lanka, Thailand, Philippines, Kenya and Mexico.[59] In some cases, these are parents who consider nothing immoral in earning income through the sex work of their children; for example in Thailand[60]. Sometimes religious factor also leads to child prostitution.

4. DOMESTIC SERVICES

Child labour in its most invisible form exists in the household sector in the form of domestic services. It has been a widely accepted practice in Asia, Africa and Latin America. Domestic servants or maids, as child labourer are known, may be divided into (*i*) wage employment, (*ii*) adopted (*iii*) bonded, (*iv*) contract employment, and (*v*) forced employment. The wage- employment may be offered directly or through agent/agency. In the cities, common form is wage-employment on monthly basis either directly or through some intermediary. In some societies children of relatives, friends or from orphanage are adopted and kept as domestic workers.[61] Similarly in Latin American countries "sham adoption of Amerindian children for domestic work"[62] results in virtual slavery where child labour is extremely poorly paid in terms of food, clothing and accommodation. The contract employment of child workers in domestic services is in fact selling the service of child by the guardian for a fixed period and salary which is usually taken in advance. Bonded child labour is the labour exacted from children to pay off some debt or advance money taken by guardians. They are not paid any remuneration till debt is not cleared and it happens very rarely. Forced employment exists in many forms. Sometimes children are kidnapped and or sold to some one for domestic work. They are not paid and forced to work till get an opportunity to be free.

Child domestic workers are paid very little. Their working hours are very long and working conditions are so poor that employers rarely provide medical care[63]. These children as domestic workers are among the most exploited of working children. No estimate could be given of child workers in domestic services but guessed that there number in Asia, Africa and Latin America may be in millions.

These are the four niches where most of the child labour exists. The formal sector in most of the countries is virtually and almost free from the use of child labour, even in developing countries. However, these are basically agricultural and allied sector and informal sector where the use of child labour is overwhelming. Though poverty is the root cause but other socio-economic, cultural and even religious factors in developing countries which have been promoting child labour. The growing disparity in a society has encouraged working children and their number is also growing despite all the child labour prevention laws. This is what is more disturbing!

REFERENCES

1. Challis, J. and D. Elliman (1979), *Child Workers Today,* Middlesex, Quarter maine House Ltd.
2. Shepherd, A.W. (1979), "The Development of Capitalist Rice Farming in Northern Ghana", Combridge, Ph.D. Dissertation.
3. Van Hear, N. (1995), "Child Labour and the Development of Capitalist Agriculture in Ghana", in Judith Ennew (ed.), *Learning or Labouring?,* Florence, UNICEF, p. 62.
4. *Ibid*, p. 63.
5. *Ibid*, p. 64.

6. ILO (1930), *Convention Concerning Forced or Compulsory Labour,* Geneva, ILO, Art. 2(1).
7. U.N. (1956), *Supplementary Convention on the Abolition of Slavery, the Slave Trade and Institutions and Practices Similar to Slavery,* Sept. 7, and enforced on April 30, 1957, 266 UNTS 3.
8. Sawyer, R. (1988), *Children Enslaved,* London, Routledge, p. 47.
9. Burra, N. (1986), "Child Labour in India: Poverty, Exploitaton and Vested Interest", *Social Action,* 36, July-Sept., p. 248.
10. Fyfe, A (1989), *Child Labour,* Oxford, Polity Press, p. 75.
11. ILO (1993), "Forced Labour" in *World Labour Report,* 1993, Geneva, ILO, p.11.
12. Anti-Slavery Society (1991), *Children in Bondage: Slaves of the Subcontinent,* London, Anti-Slavery Society, p. 24.
13. ILO (1993), *Op.cit.*
14. *Ibid*, p. 12.
15. ILO (1995), *International Child Labour Hearing,* U.S. Department of Labour, quoted in *By the Sweat & Toil of Children*, Vol. II, U.S. Deptt. of Labour, p. 21.
16. Challis, J. & D. Elliman (1979), *Op. cit.,* p. 91.
17. Bonnet, M. (1993), "Child Labour in Africa", *International Labour Review,* Vol. 132 (3), p. 382.
18. William Malya (1995), *National Programme Co-ordinator, International Programme for the Elimination of Child labour,* Dar-ES-Salaam, June 20, in an interview by Deptt. of Labour official, cited in U.S. Deptt. of labour, *op.cit,* p. 36.
19. ILO (1992), *Towards Action Against Child Labour in Zimbabwe,* Geneva, ILO, pp. 46-47.
20. NCRC/UNICEF (1993), *Children and Women in South Africa: A Situation Analysis,* Johannesburg, UNICEF.
21. Federation of Kenya Employers (1994), *Report on a Survey on Child Labour in Commercial Agricultural Plantations in Kenya,* Nairobi, Federation of Kenya Employers, p.8.
22. Onyongo, Philista, P.M. (1988), "Child Labour Policies and Programmes in Kenya", in Bequele, A & Jo Boyden (eds.), *Combating Child Labour,* Geneva, ILO, p. 162.
23. Loewenson, R. (1995), *Child Labour in Commercial Agriculture in Zimbabwe: Report of a Case Study,* Harare, IPECL (ILO) p. 8.
24. Onyango, Philista P.M. (1988), *Op.cit.*
25. UNICEF (1992), *Situation Analysis of Children and Women in Pakistan,* Islamabad, UNICEF, p. 83.
26. Bangladesh Bureau of Statistics (1992), *Report on Labour Force Survey 1989: Trend of Civilian Labour Force,* Dhaka, B.B.S. xiii, 38-39.
27. ILO (1993), *Child Labour in Indonesia*, Geneva, ILO.
28. Charoenwal, M.(1987), "Country Paper: Thailand", in PIACT (ed.), *Asian*

Regional Tripartite Workshop on Practical Measures to Combat Child Labour: Proceedings & Working Papers, Geneva, ILO, 271.

29. Bhowmit, S.K. (1992), "Plantation Labour Act and Child Labour", *Economic & Political Weekly,* vol. xxvii; 42, Oct. 17.
30. Pinlac, Amparo B. (1987), "Country Paper: Philippines", in PIACT (ed.), *op. cit.,* p. 308.
31. "Children Used to Spray Cyanide in Benguet", *Manila Chronicle,* July 27, 1992.
32. Lee-Wright, P. (1990), *Child Slaves*, London, Earthscan.
33. Jome, K.S. et. al (1993), *Child Workers in Asia,* vol. 9 : 2, Apr- June, pp. 18-19.
34. ILO (1994), *General Report and Observations Concerning Particular Countries,* Geneva, ILO, p. 135.
35. Ritcher, K. & Ard-am, O (1995), *Child Labour in Thailand's Fishing Industry*, Salaya, Nakhon Pathom, Mahidol University, Table 1,4 also pp. 16-21.
36. Van Oosterhout (1988), "Child Labour in the Philippines: The Muro-amdeep-sea fishing operation" in ILO (ed.), *Combating Child Labour, op. cit.*, p. 111.
37. Banpasirichote, B & A Pongsapich (1992), *Child Workers in Hazardous Work in Thailand*, Chulalong korn University Social Research Institute, pp. 42-46.
38. ILO (1993), *Child Labour in Indonesia,* Geneva, ILO.
39. Goonesekere, S.W.E. (1993), *Child Labour in Sri Lanka,* Geneva, ILO, pp. 9-10.
40. Centre of Concern for Child Labour (1992), *A Summary of Child Labour* Report, New Delhi, CCCL, p.4.
41. Phadke, S (1995), "Eleven-year Old Girls Gets Deliverance From Sea of Bonded Labour", *Bombay Times,* Feb. 14.
42. Human Rights Commission of Pakistan (1994), *State of Human Rights in Pakistan,* Lahore, HRCP, pp. 121-122.
43. U.N. *Document E/CN.4/sub.2/199/NGO/15,* p. 3.
44. *News from Brazil,* No. 172, Mar. 30, 1995.
45. See *Country Reports on Human Rights Practices,* U.S. Deptt. of State, Feb. 1995.
46. Children's Rights International (1990), *Children Without Childhood: Violations of Children's Right in Guatemala*, Guatemala City, C.R.I., pp. 21-22.
47. Sutton, A. (1994), *Slavery in Brazil,* London, Anti-Slavery International, p. 84.
48. Fyfe, A (1989), *op. cit.*, p. 76.
49. Challis, J & D. Elliman (1979), *op. cit.*, p. 17.
50. Schibotto, G. & A. Cussianovich (1994), *Working Children: Building an Identity,* Lima Peru, Manthoc, p. 31.

51. Glauser, B. (1990), "Street Children: Deconstructing a Construct" in James, H. & A. Prout (eds.), *Constructing and Reconstructing Childhood : Contemporary Issues in Sociological Study of Childhood,* Brighton, The Falmer Press, p. 139.
52. Ministry of Labour & Human Welfare (1999), *Situation Analysis of Street Children in Eritrea: National Survey Report,* Asmara (Eritrea), MLHW, p. 4.
53. Glauser, B. (1990), *op. cit.,* pp. 139-142.
54. Schibotto, G. & A. Cussianovich, *op. cit.,* p. 66.
55. *Ibid,* p. 25.
56. U.N. (1997), *Doc. A/49/478,* Oct, 5, p. 29.
57. Hodgson, D. (n.d.) "*Sex Tourism and Child Prostitution in Asia : Legal Responses and Strategies*", Deptt. of Law, The University of Western Australia, p. 3.
58. Dimenstein, G. (1994), "Little Girls of the Night", in *Disposable Children: The Hazards of Growing up Poor in Latin America,* vol. XXVII : 6, New York, North American Congress on Latin America, pp. 29-33.
59. ILO (1995), *In the Twilight Zone : Child Workers in the Hotel, Tourism and Catering Industry,* Geneva, ILO, pp. 8, 20-21.
60. *Ibid,* p. 30.
61. Goonesekere, S.W.E. (1993), *Child Labour in Sri Lanka; Learning from the Past,* Geneva, ILO, p. 11.
62. Challis, J. & D. Elliman (1979), *op. cit.,* p. 18.
63. Rahman, H. (1992), *Situation of Child Domestic Services,* Dhaka, UNICEF, p. 12.

5. CHILD LABOUR IN EXPORT INDUSTRIES

Child labour is used in every sector in developing countries. And export sector is no exception. Growing concern for the protection of the rights of the child and implementation of legislation in these countries coupled with the intensified efforts being made by NGOs, child labour is becoming invisible, though persists. Asia, Africa and Latin America use child labour in their export industries as comprehensively enunciated by the U.S. Department of Labour.

ASIA

Around sixty percent of total child labour is found in Asia. These countries are the most populous, poor and striving for development. Hence, export industries employ children, less on permanent basis and more as casual or contract workers, in Asian countries. India tops the list for having the largest number of child labour and export industries thrive upon the use of child labour. The most infamous is the carpet industry. Its weaving centres are scattered through out the country but concentration is found in the states of Uttar Pradesh, Jammu & Kashmir and Rajasthan. However, the carpet belt is around Mirzapur/Bhadoi in U.P. The estimates of child labour in the hand-knotted carpet industry vary from source to source however, it is in the range of 300,000 to 400,000.[1]

Children in carpet industry in India perform all the tasks. These are sorting, knotting, cutting, washing and dyeing.[2] A large number of very young children work as apprentices[3] and not paid for several years. Child labour may broadly be divided as (*i*) unpaid and (*ii*) paid workers. In the unpaid category further classification may be done : (*a*) unpaid children labouring on the family looms, (*b*) unpaid child workers working along with wage earning members of the family, and (*c*) unpaid apprentices learning skills of the trade.

The division of work in the carpet industry is either contractual or wage employment. Children like adults are paid at piece-rate and due to extremely low payment, they have to work for long-hours so that they can sustain. The manufacturer-cum-exporter distributes work through their agents who in turn assign the job to loom workers in villages or outskirts of the city. Sub-contracting is a common practice and hence children on looms in rural areas remain invisible. Child labour generally used for hand-knotting, a job which is technically considered suitable for children for their nimble fingers which can tie more knots per square inch. They work in huts where looms are established and have to sit for 12 to 18 hours in damp pits. It is indeed a bone-breaking job.

Children also work as part of the family labour. Infact work is assigned to the household head on contract or piece-rate basis. In order to earn subsistence income, children have to work on family looms and their working conditions are not as harsh as when they work on looms for the contractor or agent. However, they are unpaid workers and total earning goes to the head of the household as he is decision-making centre and commands total authority over his children.

Children in bondage is a common practice. Sub-agents recruit young children by advancing some amount to the father or guardian. The child in return has to work for long hours at nominal wage till the amount is cleared. It rarely happens due to low-wage and exploitative interest rate. Sometimes children are abducted and forced to work on looms without any payment. Though such labour is termed as forced labour but in practice it is nothing short of slavery.

Another product exported from India is brassware and base metal articles largely produced in Moradabad in Uttar Pradesh. Burra had found in her study[4] that more than 90 percent product is exported. There are some distinct characteristics of brassware industry. Firstly it comes under the category of hazardous work. Secondly, child labourers in this industry are wage labourers. Thirdly, majority of child workers come from the minority community, i.e. Muslims while most of the manufacturers and exporters are from the majority community *viz.* Hindu. Fourthly, child workers largely work for others on wages and do not work for their families. Fifthly, children perform all tasks—from standing on top of furnace and removing molten metals for electroplating and polishing. It has been estimated that nearly forty five thousand children work in Moradabad based brassware factories. However, if the work in the neighbouring villages is taken into account, number of children working in brassware industry may go up atleast by ten percent.

Gem polishing industry largely located in Jaipur, Rajasthan and Surat, Gujarat in India has been thriving on child labour. These are basically diamonds processed and polished in Surat, and emeralds polished in Jaipur which are exported. The number of working children are 'guesstimated' between 6000 and 100,000.

The case of child labour in the diamond cutting industry in Surat has been highlighted by the ORG[5] in 1993, where children between the age of 12 and 13 years work for long hours under unhygienic condition and are underpaid. Gem polishing industries and the use of child labour therein has been highlighted by Burra[6], who studied Gem polishing industry in Jaipur. Children belonging to labourer families and of low income groups generally work in the Gem polishing industry of Jaipur. The former fall in the age group of 6 to 10 years while the latter being school going children belong to 10-14 years age group. The entire Gem polishing is done by children under 14 years of age.[7] The apprenticeship system also exists in which apprentices are not paid during their training except for some occasional pocket money.

Glass and glassware industry in Firozabad (U.P.) also employs a large number of children under 18 years of age. Like Gem polishing industry, no estimate of child labour is available except 'guesstimate' of 8 to 50 thousand.[8] These factories manufacture glass bangles, wine glasses, beads, chandeliers, bulb and crockery and scientific glass products for the use in science laboratories. The work is so hazardous that it has been compared with Dante's inferno[9] due to the furnance temperature between 1400 and 1600 Celsius.

Less attention has been paid to the sequine work industry[10] generally known in India as Zari/Zardozi mainly concentrated in the towns of Bareilly, Rampur, Shahjahanpur, Lucknow, Varanasi in Uttar Pradesh, and Bhopal in Madhya Pradesh. A large number of young boys and girls work in this industry and are paid on piece-rate basis. Sequine work based apparels and garments are exported to a number of countries e.g. U.S.A., Israel, Middle-East countries, worth millions of dollars.

The *modus operandi* of exporters is complex. They are generally based in the capital city and procure orders from abroad. Then the work is assigned along with samples to the agent who happens to be a craftman. The craftman in turn contacts his sub-agents and provides all the material, e.g. cloth, beads etc. along with designs. These are handed over to local sub-agents who distribute work among the workers. Children work on cloth fixed to a wooden frame and do the needle work. They are paid through the chain of agents and payment is generally on piece-rate basis. In some cases, children work in the *Karkhana* (factory) from morning till evening and get remuneration on work basis.

Children are under paid and work places are invariably unhygienic as these lack proper light and ventilation. In the whole process, these are workers including children who are under paid. The exporters get maximum, then the contractor who is generally craftman pockets the rest. From workers share, a large portion is pocketed by sub-agents who get work done. It's a back-breaking work and workers are generally indebted to the sub-contractors who, in turn, remain indebted to the main contractor.

The U.S. Embassy in New Delhi informed the U.S. Department of Labour about footwear industry in India exporting $107 million in 1993 worth of footwear to the United States that "child labour is known or widely believed to be used in the shoe export industry".[11] It is estimated that there are 25,000 children working in the Indian footwear industry.[12]

There is 'sub-contract system' which absorbs child labour. The contractor of the firm distributes work to the workers at their homes where children between 10-15 years in majority do soling with glue. The workers under unhygienic conditions and due to continuous contact with industrial adhesive suffer from skin and breathing diseases. Most of the shoe manufacturing work in India is concentrated around Agra and Kanpur in Uttar Pradesh.

Pyrotechnics and match-making industry located mainly in Sivakasi where children are largely employed, somewhere between 50,000 and 100,000 and industry is thriving on child labour.[13] The estimated number of match units is around 3000 where 55 percent are working children under 14 years of age.[14] Moreover, there are around 300 licensed fire works factories while the number of unlicensed runs into several hundreds and estimated number of working children is between 30 to 70 thousand. Their working hours are as long as 12 hours where children handle from dying of paper to rolling gum powder and using chemical. These are all hazardous work. It has also been observed that children working in tiny units or unlicensed ones get less piece rate than their counterparts in big or licensed units.

There are a large number of other industries like silk, handloom and handicrafts industries where child labour is being largely used and their products are being exported. It is, however, difficult even to 'guesstimate' the number of children working exclusively for exports as domestic production is not clearly segregated.

It is an interesting fact that all the child labour in export sector is confined to the garment industry in Bangladesh. There are 1800 garment factories registered with Bangladesh Garment Manufacturers & Exporters Association (BGMEA) while number of workers is reported to be 800,000 where females are of all child workers under 14 years.[17] The number of child workers is controversial ranging between 8000 to 550,000 but it is guesstimate that if sub-contracting units are taken into account, then the number of child workers would not be less than 50,000. And it is conformed by the fact that due to the Child Labour Deterrence Act, employers dismissed an estimated 50,000 children from the factories in 1993 which is stated to be 75 percent of child labour. It means child labour in the garment industries had been well above 50,000.

The working conditions are sub-standard as children in multi storied factory buildings work under oppressively hot conditions for 10 to 14 hours per day, usually locked from outside and have no break during the shift, and being unskilled are paid less.

It is apprehended that most of the dismissed child workers must have joined unlicensed units and are invisible child labour. However, no follow-up study has been conducted to ascertain the fact.

Child labour is being used in the export sector not only by Indonesian factories but many foreign firms based in Indonesia also use cheap child labour to manufacture semi-finished products for export. KOMPAK had reported in 1991 that children under 14 years work in the export factories of Tangerang and their working conditions are very poor as child workers are paid meagre wage-rate and have to work from 7 to 13 hours per day, seven days per week.[18]

Indonesia has a number of export industries but prominent ones are rapidly growing export oriented *rattan* furniture industry located in Tegalwani, Cirebon where largely children under 14 are employed. There are three categories of child workers (*i*) paid helpers, (*ii*) wage-earners, and (*iii*) apprentices where the last category, i.e. apprentice is a source of cheap labour.[19] Not only rattan but also other furniture industry like 'reproductions' in Jepara in Central Java relies on child labour.

Another export industry in Indonesia is garments and textile industry where children work. However, no estimate of working children is available while total working children between 10 and 14 years are reported to be 2.2 million i.e. 3 percent of total labour force.[20]

NEPAL

Nepal is one of the poor countries in Asia and the world and hence a direct relationship between poverty and child labour may be assumed safely. There is not much export from Nepal except that of carpets as a significant item. Child Workers in Nepal Concerned Centre (CWIN) studied carpet industries in 1992 and estimated that in 2000 odd carpet factories around 150,000 children are working in the age group of 11-14 year.[21]

In Nepal, just like India, carpet industry gets most of child labour through agents known as Naike. These children are generally recruited from the interior and poverty striken villages and forced to work for 15 hours a day, on an average and receive meagre wages.[22] These working children are usually bonded and exploited not only economically but even sexually.[23] Hence working conditions for children in carpet industries in Nepal are exploitative and extremely poor.

Another Asian country where child labour is prominently exploited in employment is Pakistan. Child labour has assumed a massive proportion due to (*i*) large number of working children under 10 and 10-14 years and (*ii*) practice of bonded labour. It is estimated that the number of working children in the age-group 10-14 years is around two million as per the Pakistan Labour Force Survey of 1990-91, while UNICEF's estimate is 8 million.[24]

Capret industry is one of those in Pakistan which prominently uses child labour. According to the UNICEF report there are one million child workers in the carpet industry of Pakistan.[25] Child labour is thriving in carpet industry since 90 percent looms are in the villages where children work as part of the family labour. Moreover, weaving units being home based fall in the category of cottage industry where labour laws are not applicable. These children are either uneducated or school drop-out. Moreover, in violation of Bonded Labour Abolition Act of 1992, children working in the carpet industry are bonded through *peshgi*[26] (advance) system. A majority of children working in carpet industry is male and paid on job-basis. The working conditions are poor at home and in the weaving centres. In order to avoid labour regulations, manufacturers usually follow sub-contracting where middlemen act as a link between the manufacturer and home-based weavers. Moreover, large firms divide their enterprise into smaller units so as to escape the labour laws which are applicable in units employing more than 10 workers. Child labour is more in the rural areas where most of the looms are established in the weavers' homes and there children have to work for longer hours than those in the urban workshops or factories. Their work as described by the UNICEF is painful for children as they have to "sit in cramped positions for long periods of time, breathing wool dust, working under poor lighting conditions, straining their eyes and working with chemical dyes. These children also develop spinal deformities."[27]

Soccer ball industry mainly located around Sialkot in Pakistan produced around seventy five percent of the World's total output in 1996. Child labour used in the soccer ball industry in Sialkot region is estimated around 7000 between the ages of 5 and 14 years working on full time basis for stitching.[28] These children usually work for 8 to 9 hours in their homes and hence they are invisible. On an average a child stitches one to five balls per day and average payment per ball is 20 to 22 rupees.[29] The practice of child labour in debt bondage is also prevalent in the soccer ball industry in Pakistan.[30]

There are some other export industry in Pakistan, for example, sport goods and surgical instruments where child labour is used.

Those countries where child labour has become a massive problem include the Philippine. Estimate is that around 5 million children are working in the country and it coincides with the ILO and the UNICEF estimates. The main export industries where child labour is used on a large scale are: garments, furniture and gold mining. This is the garment industry which largely employs children. To avoide labour laws it has a sub-contract system where children work at home or make-shift work places.[31] They are paid on piece-work basis which is invariably less than the legal minimum wage. They are exploited further for they pay all expenses for needles, threads and even repairing of machines[32] which reduces their net payment or what in economics is called as money wages. Child labour figures for the garments exporting industry are not available.

In the wood and rattan furniture industry, which is export oriented more children work in industrial establishments rather than at homes for sub-contractors.[33]

In gold mining, packers are young boys and they get attracted by the remuneration paid to them as they easily earn between 40 and 50 peso every day. They carry the bags of ore down the hill in the South Catabato region and children have left their school to become packers.[34]

The ILO has reported a figure of four million children working in Thailand while 600,000 are between the ages of 13 and 14 years.[35] Similarly, the UNICEF has reported a government survey of 1986 which found 1.05 million children between 11-14 years of age, while 124,000 were in the age group of 11 and 12 years.[36] Child labour is used in garments, gems, leather, seafood processing and furniture industries. All these are export industries. In the garment industry, child labour is used in sub-contracted sweatshops or in small units in the Pratunam district in Bangkok. Children are hired for work through agents or 'shops' on commission basis and migrant children work under appalling conditions.[37] Since mostly work in 'underground' sweatshop factories, their estimation is difficult.

Gems industry is also a foreign exchange earner in Thailand, especially its Khon Khaen area where children are used for gem polishing. Most of child labour works either in small sheds called 'neighbourhood' factories or at home under sub-contract given to families. Other urban centres as Chaing Mai in Bangkok get the supply of labour from poverty striken northeastern region through recruiting agents. During the period of training, no wages are paid and working conditions are extremely poor.

Thailand exports rattan, wicker, straw, cane, palm and buri furniture to many countries including the USA. In the furniture industry including wood, child labour is commonly used. However, 'underground' sweatshop factories make child labour invisible.

Asian countries have more child workers than the countries of any other region and export industries are thriving on child labour facilitated by sub-contracting or bondage system prevailing in all the countries of the region. Export sector is no exception.

LATIN AMERICA

Brazil, fifth largest country having population which is seventh largest population in the world is also known for the problem of working children in general and, street children in particular. The economy is infected with child labour. And so are the export industries, e.g. textile and garments, footwear, leather processing, handicrafts etc.

The ILO has reported that there are 17 percent of total child labour force in the textile and garment sector[38]. A Government sponsored survey of child labour in 1990 revealed that over 50 percent children under 14 years of age work in the garment and textile industry. However, lack of proper documentation of working children inhibits definite or estimated statistics of child labour in this sector.

Brazil exports shoes as one of the leading item where incidentally children under 14 years largely work. Shoe work is concentrated in Franca and has been studied concerning with the use of child labour[39]. The shoes industry has sub-contracting system and that is how the child labour is conveniently used. Out of seven thousand sub-contracted workers there were 1300 children under 14 years of age, i.e. 18.5 per cent of total labourers. These children work for contractors at their homes or in workplaces devoid of even basic facilities such as garages or verandas etc; where they do all sorts of work ranging from cutting and trimming to hand-sewing and gluing. Not only working conditions are deplorable but children get exposed to hazards such as toxic and addictive fumes of glue leading to many health problems and diseases.

One of primary exports of Brazil is tin which is mined in the state of Rondonia. Anti-Slavery organization has reported that around 17 percent of total labourers working at the mine were children and adolescents.[40] In short, mining work at Bom Futuro actually violates human rights[41] where children are exploited.

In most cases, sub-contracting becomes a shield and labour

laws do not reach such places hence exploitation of child labour continues.

Colombia's one of the primary export industry is floriculture or flower industry located largely in the Bogota plateau where around 85 percent of total 300 large enterprises exist. Cut flower industry has a large labour force of 140,000 and guesstimate of child workers is around 25 percent.

How the child labour got entry into the flower industry? There has been a rapid growth around plantations mainly habitated by poor families. Therefore, over population, poverty and lack of educational facilities, breaking of family led children to supplement family income by working in the flower plantations. Salazar's study[42] seems to be only source providing scanty account of child labour in cut flowers' export industry.

Coal mining is another major export industry of Columbia where informal mining account for the bulk of total output. These mining units heavily rely on manual work and hence provide employment to children at low wages. Most of the young child miners are migrants from rural areas and perform various tasks ranging from carrying water out to digging charcoal inside the mine and loading the packs on the mules. Their families encourage children for working in the mines rather than attending school.

Leather is also exported from Columbia, while leather tanning is largely confined to cottage industries sector having outdated and manual technology and hence requires unskilled labour. Children do fit in there first as apprentices at the age of 5 or 6 years and not being paid during the period of their training. Older children are employed as paid labourers and they are between 12-14 years, they perform all sorts of work as they become skilled workers. Their work is hazardous as dying requires handling of chemicals. It is exploitative for they work long hours, i.e. up to nine hours for meagre payment while working conditions are unhygienic and poor.

The assembling units called '*maquiladoras*' usually assemble transportation equipment, electrical and electronic goods, furniture and sport goods etc. and export from Mexico. Such exporting units are situated in the border region of Mexico and

U.S.A. This region has attracted large number of families in search of work where educational and other facilities are lacking. Hence, children get drifted into work. These are generally girls in their early teenage who get job in maquildoras and have to work under harsh conditions. No thorough documentation of child labour in assembling- export units is available. However the use of child labour there has been conformed by certain studies conducted in such regions.

Similarly, one-tenth of economically active 12-15 year children work in palm leaf and wood crafts falling under the category of handicrafts. Shoe export industry is no exception and it uses child labour, particularly in Guanajuato state of Mexico.[43]

AFRICA

Not much work has been done on the problem of child labour in Africa. Very few countries have been touched upon to study the problem in the context of industry and mining and rare are the studies on export industry. It is mainly due to reasons that (*i*) no literature is available and (*ii*) export industry is still nascent in this region. However, the region has been exporting gold and diamonds and other minerals.

Cote d' Ivoire has gold mines at Issia and diamond mine at Tortiya. A joint report[44] of the UNICEF and Defense for Children International revealed the use of child labour in the central-west region, which is a forested area. Since family labour is generally working in the gold mines, children get drifted into the work as neither education nor recreation options are available to them. There is no working facilities and rudimentary tools are used. Children do all kinds of mining work, ranging from digging to cleaning the rocks etc. Their average age has been stated around seven years.[45] Working conditions are extremely poor and exploitative.

Similarly, in the northern region of the country diamond mines are located around Tortiya. The UNICEF/DCI reported around 350 child workers in diamond mining as part of the family labour but the U.S. team did not find more than five or six children when it visited in 1994.[46] It shows that mining in Cote d'

Ivoire uses child labour but it is not a serious problem and could be dealt with effectively.

Egypt in northern Africa is a major country where child labour proportions and problem are serious. Small-scale export industries in Egypt use child labour, particularly in carpet, leather textile, and garment industries. Traditional carpet industry generally known as hand-knotted do use child labour. It has been found during the course of survey that children between the ages of 10 and 14 years work and are disguised as practice loom apprentices which is not true. They have been found working for 10 hours a day. Moreover, sub-contracting of weaving to the rural artisans also promotes the use of child labour due to invisibility. No effort, however, has been reported to estimate the proportion of child labour except estimating 22 per cent share of 12 to 14 year age group in total work.[47]

Leather tanning industry has been reported [48] to use child labour and it is conformed for domestic sector, however, indirectly child labour may have been used by the export industry. Children work irregular hours to 'supplement' family income in small workshops. The final product passes through different stages involving sub-contracting, hence establishing a direct link between the use of child labour and exports becomes difficult.

Egypt has a large number of small-scale textile units where child labour prevails. A survey[49] of 100 such small factories and family operated workshops, producing half of the textile products, revealed the use of child labour to the extent of one-fourth of the total labour force used there. Working conditions for children in these small-scale units flout labour laws of the country. Another study[50] establishes a definite relationship between school dropout and working children in small-scale industries, some of which are supplier to large firms which, in turn, export to other countries.

Analogously another country in Northern Africa, i.e., Morocco uses child labour in its carpet industry, which is export oriented. The number of child workers under 14 in the export-oriented carpet industry has been estimated between two and three thousand.[51] It has been conformed by other sources that under 14 child workers are there in the carpet export industry some where between 5 and 10 percent of total labour force in this particular export industry.[52]

Garment's exports contribute nearly one-fifth of Morocco's total exports. Under sub-contracting system, child labour is used in small workshops. Child workers under 10 years of age are generally assigned light work such as, clipping threads and folding etc. in these small units supplying to large firms for exports.

Leather tanning largely producing for domestic consumption and small-scale exports to Northern Africa uses child labour in workshops where working conditions are quite poor in terms of wages and facilities. Here apprenticeship seems to be at the core leading to exploitation of children.[53]

Lesotho is one of those African countries experiencing a surge in its exports of garments, especially apparel and clothing accessories since 1989. The use of child labour in garment export industry is significant since 5 to 15 percent of the total workforce are children in the age group of 12-15 years. Even foreign owned companies in Lesotho assembling garments for export use child labour for cutting, sewing and packing. Child workers are generally paid a minimum wage.

In case of other industries like leather and shoe, no direct evidence is possible due to sub-contracting system prevailing there. However, the Employment Act of 1977 prohibits children under 15 years of age in the industry and commercial undertakings in Lesotho.[54]

An ILO study[55] establishes the use of child labour atleast in two export-oriented operations in Zimbabwe. These are chrome units which due to very low price settings use cheap child labour. Children living in co-operatives work along with their parents and it is feared that "the increased use of children in chrome mining has been a direct, if unintended, consequence of government"[56] which promoted the use of cooperatives.

Gold panning has become a good source of income in Zimbabwe and is one of largest sources of income. As per the U.S. report[57] Associated Mineworkers Union claims that some 500,000 are working in gold mining. Since more panners result in more gold, children are also engaged in panning of gold. These are basically independent mine operators who promote the use of child labour in contravention to the industry agreement that under 17 years may not be employed in the mining operations in Zimbabwe.

African countries do not have many export industries, however child labour is prevalent in export or export-oriented industries.

REFERENCES

1. U.S. Deptt. of Labour (1994), *By the Sweat & Toil of Children,* Washington D.C., p. 74.
2. Vijaygopalan, S. (1993), *Child Labour in the Carpet Industry: A Status Report,* New Delhi, NCAER, pp. 43-44.
3. Gupta, M. & K.Voll (1987), *Young Hands at Work,* New Delhi, Atma Rama & Sons, p. 49.
4. Burra, N. (1989), *Child Labour in the Brassware Industry of Moradabad,* ILO/Asian Regional Team for Employment Promotion, p. 15.
5. Operations Research Group (1993), *Child Labour in Different Industries: Consolidated Report,* Madras (Chennai).
6. Burra, N. (1991), *Child Labour in the Gem Polishing Industry in Jaipur,* Noida (U.P.), N.L.I., Child Labour Cell.
7. *Ibid*, p.11.
8. U.S. Deptt. of Labour (1994), *op. cit.,* p. 81.
9. *Ibid*, p. 82.
10. *Based on Observations in Bareilly and nearby towns where the author resides. All details of modus operandi were provided by the contractor by the name of Naeem who himself has become an exporter.*
11. U.S. Deptt. of Labour (1994), *op. cit.,* p. 83.
12. *Ibid.*
13. Dingwaney, M.et. al (1988), *Children of Darkness : A Manual on Child Labour in India,* New Delhi, N.L.I., p. 8.
14. ICFTU-APRO (1992), *Pilot Study of Child Labour in Sivakasi*, New Delhi, ICFTU- A PRO, South Asia Office, p. 4.
15. Mahajan, K. & J. Gathia (1992), *Child Labour : An Analytical Study,* New Delhi, CCCL, p. 27.
16. ICFTU- APRO (1992), *op. cit.*
17. U.S. Deptt. of Labour (1994), *op. cit.,* p. 28 ff.
18. As cited in the U.S. Deptt. of Labour (1994), *op. cit.,* p. 95.
19. White, B.& I. Tjandraningsih (n.d.), *Rural Children in the Industrialization Process: Child and Youth Labour in 'Traditional' and 'Modern' Industries*

in West Java, (mss), pp. 19-20 as cited in U.S. Deptt. of Labour (1994), *op. cit.*, p. 96.

20. UNICEF (1993) , *Situation Analysis on Women and Children in Indonesia,* New York, Unicef, p. 252.
21. CWIN (n.d.), "*Carpet Factory : A Source of Foreign Currency and the Misery of Our Children*", Kathmandu, CWIN, (brochure).
22. Pradhan, G. (1993), *Misery Behind the Looms; Child Labourers in the Carpet Factories in Nepal,* Kathmandu, CWIN, pp. 19, 26.
23. *Ibid*, p. 29.
24. U.S. Deptt of Labour (1994), *op.cit.,* p. 126 ff No. 2.
25. UNICEF (1992), *Child Labour in the Carpet Weaving Industry in Punjab,* Punjab (Pakistan), UNICEF, p. 7.
26. AAFLI (1994), *A Report on Child Labour in Pakistan,* Asian-American Free Labour Institute, pp. 5-6.
27. U.S. Deptt. of Labour (1994), *op. cit.,* p. 130.
28. Directorate of Labour Welfare & IPEC (1996), *Child Labour in the Football Manufacturing Industry,* Geneva, ILO, p. iv.
29. Raasta (1996), *An Assessment of the Working Child in the Soccer Ball Industry*, Lahore, Raasta Development Consultants, p. 19.
30. *Ibid*, p. ix.
31. Macaranas, J. (1994), *Child Labour in The Philippines,* Washington D.C., ILRERF, pp. 5-6.
32. Rasario, del R. (1990), *Sub-contracting Networks in the Garment Industry in Taytay and Angono*, Rizal, Manila, The Philippine University/ UNICEF, p. 11.
33. U.S. Deptt: of Labour (1994), *op.cit.,* p. 139, referring to the ILO Study of 1988 .
34. *Ibid*, p. 140.
35. ILO (1994), *Report of the Committee of Experts on the Application of Conventions and Recommendations : General Report and Observations Concerning Particular Countries,* Geneva, ILO, p. 135.
36. UNICEF (1989), "*Thai Children At Work*", in *The Situation Analysis for Women and Children*, New York, UNICEF, p. 27.
37. Ennew, J &B. Milne (1989), *The Next Generation: Lives of Third World Children*, London, Zed Books Ltd., pp. 173-174.
38. ILO (1988), *Committee of Experts Report*, Geneva, ILO, p. 53.
39. Pereira, I. & R.L.B. Rosa (1993) , *Child Labour in the Footwear Industry in Franca,* Geneva, ILO.
40. Sutton, A. (1994), *Slavery in Brazil,* London, Anti-Slavery International, p. 93.
41. *Ibid.*
42. Slazar, Maria Cristina *et. al* (1994), Child Labour in Industrial Sectors in Colombia, Santafe de Bogota, cited in U.S. Deptt. of Labour (1994), *op. cit.*, pp. 50-51.

43. U.S. Deptt. of Labour (1994), *op. cit.*, p. 109.
44. Kponhassia, G. (1993), *Child Labour in the Mines of Cote d' Ivoire (in french) New York*, UNICEF/DCI, pp. 6-8, cited in the U.S. Deptt. of Labour, *op. cit*, p. 58-59.
45. *Ibid.*
46. Deptt. of Labour (1994), *op. cit.*, p. 59, ff. no. 6.
47. *Ibid*, p. 62.
48. Abdallah, A. (1988), "Child Labour in Egypt: Leather Tanning in Cairo", in Alec fyfe, *Combating Child Labour*, Geneva, ILO, pp. 33-34.
49. Azer, A. *et al.* (1993), *Training and Welfare of Working Children in Shubra El Kheima*, Cairo, ILO/NCSCR.
50. Azer, A. (1990), *Child Labour in Egypt*, Cairo, UNICEF/ NCSCR.
51. U.S. Deptt. of Labour (1994), *op.cit.*, citing letter from UMT to International Child Labour Study (June 22), p. 114.
52. Guessous, S.N. (1994), *The Use of Child Labour in Morocco in the Production of Goods Exported to the United States*, Casablanca, cited in the U.S. Deptt. of Labour, *op.cit.*
53. U.S. Deptt. of Labour (1994), *op. cit.*, pp. 115-116.
54. UNICEF (1991), *The Situation of Women and Children in Lesotho*, Maseru, Ministry of Planning, Economic and Manpower, in Collaboration with UNICEF, p. 127.
55. ILO (1992), *Towards Action Against Child Labour in Zimbabwe*, Geneva, ILO.
56. U.S. Deptt. of Labour (1994), *op. cit.*, p. 164.
57. *Ibid*, ff p. 165.

6. REGION THAT WARRANTS MORE ATTENTION

African continent is least developed due to geographic and socio-economic constraints. So are the countries of Africa. The problem of child labour exists here in different forms and sectors. But much work has not been carried out in this direction.[1] Hence, neither quantitative nor qualitative information pertaining to socio-economic aspects exists on the problem of child labour in Africa. "Unlike Asia, research on child labour in Africa is meagre..."[2]. Most of the researchers have concluded that "a brief survey of the literature on Africa, for example, yields virtually no data"[3]. Now the question is how to study the problem of child labour in Africa when information has not been gathered and analyzed? It is not that the area is totally barren since scattered information is available. Hence, the task is to conjecture a picture of the problem with scattered information on various aspects of child labour in Africa.

CONCEPT OF CHILD IN AFRICA

Let us begin with the perception of child in Africa. The first and the foremost characteristic of the African society is that its organization is always based on clans or lineage. In such social organization of the society, members of a group are related with each other through some common ancestor, i.e. the lineage. The society may be patrilineal or matrilineal and reproductive function can be performed by two individuals. However, unlike the Western society accepting biological descent, many people may be at the same time, play the role of the parents of the same child and at the same time, i.e. the child's care is taken by the family and the community and not just by the parental couple. This causes an important distinction that the "child is not the consequence of a marriage, but rather a condition of alliance"[4]. Moreover, the family is for the child exclusively either paternal or the maternal lineage. All these factor actually define not only the social but also familial framework of a child in a traditional African society which, in turn, determines the place of a child.

There are two principal phases which may be identified from the age of three years approximately. These are age group up to seven years and seven to sixteen years. All the activities of a child, during the first phase, remain confined to the household work such as taking care of siblings younger than the child, assisting in cooking, maintenance of the living area, supply of fuel and water, harvest transport, hunting, fishing, marketing of produce and hut construction etc. In short, child participates in all the subsistence activities. However, the child is generally helped by the adults in carrying out all the subsistence activities. While in the second phase a child has activities spread over the whole area of the village, that is no more confined to subsistence activities but introduced into the productive sector as an outcome of a socialization strategy. It is also important to note that schooling does not release a child from duties in rural family communities, that is, tasks are reorganized rather reduced, giving birth to the age classes. Moreover, "relatives between age classes are an important aspect of the structure of economic activity".[5] However gender differentiation is invariably made during the second phase of a child, that is, after seven years of age and it leads to differentiation in their roles. In a nutshell, child in an African society gets integrated into subsistence and economic activities as well at an early stage.

THE NICHES OF EMPLOYMENT

(i) Agriculture

The niches of employment in African countries are agriculture i.e. their traditional channel and informal sector which is urban oriented. Most of the countries in Africa have subsistence or family farming due to geographic and harsh climatic conditions. Socio-economic institutions have also helped in this regard since child labour has been accepted in this region as an "integral part of the economic and social pattern of life"[6]. Keeping in view the social fabric of the society, child labour may be divided into (*i*) unpaid family labour, (*ii*) hired and paid labour as substitute, and (*iii*) wage employment on either per diem or contract. These categories have been formed on the basis of existing practices in the agricultural sector, though these practices vary from country to country. However, an attempt at generalization may be made.

Children in rural areas, in accordance with tradition, work alongwith their family members on subsistence farm. It is such a common practice that "children acting as unpaid family helpers can be found all over Africa".[7] This practice of using child labour as unpaid family helper has been observed in Lesotho, Botswana, Burundi, Ethiopia, Eritrea, Somalia and almost all the countries in the African continent. The situation slightly differs in the case of pastoral nomadic societies in Africa like those in northern Kenya, southern Ethiopia and Somalia etc. In a predominantly nomadic society, there is generally labour shortage keeping in view the size and diversity of herds. As is the case with *Gabra* nomads in northern Kenya and southern Ethiopia, where children are fully employed[8]. In the first phase or age group, that is, upto seven years, children live around the camp where they learn by assisting elders about looking after the animals, i.e. feeding, watering, treating sick ones and helping to milk. While in the second phase, that is, seven years onwards, children herd their stock, live away from the main homestead during the dry season. It is a sort of gradual integration into adult work but without remuneration or as unpaid workers.

The same has been observed about nomads around *Labgar* where young children till the age of ten start working in *'daral'*, i.e. cattle-pen, watch the calves before and after milking[9]. They are engaged in productive work so as to integrate them with adult work. Their tasks get differentiated on sex basis at the age of ten when boys gradually specialize in sheep and goat breeding. They perform pastoral tasks in the proximity of "*ruumande*" village while in dry season they move with their cattles towards river valley or converge on the bore-hole in *Labgar*[10] and hence are graduated to adult work.

Other responsibilities of children are watering the cattle and also fetching potable water. So the use of child labour is common for pastoral work. Children work from the very young age by assisting adults and then at the age of ten start mending cattle. In all these economic activities, children are unpaid family labourers.

In some countries such as Egypt and Sudan, small farmers hire children on wage while they themselve earn higher wages elsewhere[11]. These children are employed to pick cotton, weed and perform other tasks as substitute labourers. They are paid less than what adults get some where else. However it is not a feature common to all countries in Africa.

Children are also hired on wages either daily or for a period on contract at a fixed daily wage-rate. This is true about plantations in various African countries. Coffee plantations in Kenya, Madagascar and Uganda hire children on wages. Similarly, sisal plantation in Tanzania, Kenya; tea plantation in Kenya, Zimbabwe offer wage employment to children but a casual workers. Such children fall in the category of wage employment.

In the late sixties certain countries like Ghana experienced capitalistic agriculture which is in common parlance, known as commercial agriculture. It gave rise to wage employment of children either on daily or contract basis. Otherwise children used to work only on plantations, e.g. cocoa plantation in Ghana. With the advent of commercial farmig on a limited scale due to geographic conditions, demand for child labour on wage employment has arisen in some African countries.

(ii) Informal Sector

Another bastion of child labour in developing countries is the informal sector. How is the structure of informal sector in Africa? It needs some in-depth study.

The process of urbanization and migration from rural to

urban areas have led to the expansion of the informal sector in African countries as well which is presumed to provide more employment than the formal sector. What are the characteristics of the informal sector in Africa? These may be divided into micro and macro characteristics. The micro characteristics of the informal sector in Africa have been analyzed in terms of (*a*) size of operation, (*b*) capital-intensity, (*c*) enterpreneurship, and (*d*) apprentice system[12].

(a) Size of Operation

The average firm is either one man firm or employs two to three apprentices. However, size of operation may be judged from the following table:

Size of operation

No. of workers per:	
All establishment	3.8
Services	4.7
Production	3.9
Construction	9.5
Distribution:	
62% employ	< 5 persons
33% employ	5-10 persons
5% employ	> 10 persons

Source: *Jobs & Skills Programme for Africa/ ILO, Ababa, 1984.*

The highest concentration is of those establishments employing persons between 0-5 while activity wise, this is the construction which has largest size of operation since its establishments have an average of more than ten persons in employment.

(b) Capital Intensity

The informal sector in all developing countries as well as in Africa is characterized by labour- intensive mode of production. It is because a fraction of investment in the informal sector creates much more job opportunities as compared to the formal sector. It is estimated that an investment of one million shillings in Nairobi may create 5500 jobs in the informal sector while the same investment in the formal sector could generate employment only one-tenth of the informal sector[13]. The average capital required for workers in the informal sector is less than what is needed in the formal sector, as may be seen from the following table:

Capital per worker

Place	*Year*	*U.S. $*
Djibouti	1982	477.8
Lome	1977	161.9
Yaounde	1977	355.2
Bamako	1977	86.3
Nuakchott	1977	293.9
Kigali	1977	248.7
Kumasi	1976	203.4
Freetown	1976	42.3
Kano	1976	277.4
Nairobi	1972	25.5

Source: JASPA/ILO, Addis Ababa, 1984.

The informal sector requires much less average capital distribution over workers than the formal sector. For example, capital required per worker in the informal sector in Nairobi was 182 schillings while for the formal sector it came to 2000 schillings. Hence low capital-labour ratio is there in the informal sector of Africa. It is, therefore, easy to enter the informal sector rather than the formal sector in Africa.

It is also characteristic that capital goods produced in the informal sector of Africa are the outcome of labour-intensive technology adopted to produce 'labour saving' or 'strain saving' simple tools for the use in the sector itself[14]. Hence, the technology is not only adopted but is converted to labour-intensity as well. It has not, hence adversely affected employment in the informal sector.

(c) The entrepreneurship

The entrepreneurship has two components (*i*) capital access and (*ii*) skills . Another characteristic of the informal sector at micro level is the use of personal savings or borrowing from informal sources, such as, family borrowings, traditional sources and some funding by institutions and banks. Following table explains access to capital in the informal sector of Africa.

Source of Capital

Sources	*Percentage*
Personal Savings	73
Family / Relative	14
Traditional Market Loans	10
Institutions	03
Total	100

Source: JASPA/ILO, Addis Ababa, 1984.

As it is in any developing country of Asia, the most important source of capital funds in the informal sector of Africa is personal savings which is almost three-fourth of total capital fundings. Then comes the share of personal borrowings, i.e. loans from family members, relatives and friends. However, it is only 14 percent of total capital invested in the informal sector. The shares of market loans and formal institutions are 10 and 3 percent respectively. The contribution of banks and other financial institutions is expected to be less keeping in view the nature of entities in the sector. These are not regulated by the governments and hence not entitled for funding by the banks etc.

Secondly, entrepreneurs in the informal sector of Africa do not acquire skills in a formal way from schools and training centres. They usually have on-the-job training and become skilled. Some of them who come from the formal sector and establish their own units in the informal sector, they have acquired skill while working in the formal sector. However, there is a traditional preference for acquiring skills in the sector itself. Very few entrepreneur receive training formally and establish their own units in the informal sector. However, a distinct feature of entrepreneurship in the informal sector of Africa, like Asian countries, is the one man show as entrepreneur acquires skills as well as capital and therefore, once the entrepreneur is gone, the unit or firm becomes non-existent.

Most of the units in the informal sector have, short life span i.e. less than five years as indicated by JASPA estimates presented below:

Life span of units in the informal sector in Africa

Place	*Mean (years)*	*S.D.*
Freetown	3.7	1.9
Kumasi	4.1	1.3
Lagos	3.3	1.2
Bamako	6.3	5.0
Kigali	6.1	5.8
Lome	6.7	6.8
Nouakchott	4.7	3.1
Yaounde	3.9	3.6
Djibouti	4.5	-

Source: JASPA/ILO, Addis Ababa, 1984.

The short life span of units in the informal sector results in the loss of skill accumulation about production, sourcing of product and inputs which are largely required in Africa. Hence, economy suffers in a significant manner.

But what are the reasons for short life span of units in the informal sector? One obvious reason is the limited or small-size of market which can not support a large number of units due to easy entry and no legal restrictions. Secondly, inter-sectoral and intra-sectoral competition, which is intensive, leads to closure of many units not capable of sustaining themselve. Thirdly, units operating in the informal sector receive no support either from the government or from financial institutions. Fourthly, ploughing-back of profit is so nominal that the units fail to survive in the long-run. Fifthly, lack of marketing also leads to closure of many units in the informal sector.

Conversely what are the factor which sustain a unit in the informal sector. These are: (*i*) innovativeness due to any reason, such as, competition, (*ii*) financial adequacy due to, say, regular ploughing-back of profit, (*iii*) minimization of cost because of either better sourcing of inputs or any other reason, and (*iv*) intelligent marketing strategy mainly because of better access to the market information. Hence, those units in the informal sector which fail on any of the above listed counts cease to exist.

(d) Apprenticeship

Large number of units in the informal sector are single owner unit of a small-size and unable to afford hired labour. Most of the self-employment units have these two distinct features: (*i*) single owner and (*ii*) small-size of operation and hence can not hire a helping hand on wage employment. Such units therefore depend on the apprentices seeking the acquisition of skill of a particular trade or profession. These are usually parents who persuade for apprenticeship as shown by the cases of Ghana and Nigeria where 70 to 80 and 63 percent respectively apprentices have joined the profession since parents could not afford their education.[15]

What is apprentice system? Why is it so dominant in the informal sector? The apprentice system is a means of acquiring skills or know-how of a trade or occupation. It trains new-comers desirous of seeking not only acquisition of skills, a short-term objective but also gainful employment, i.e, the long-term objective. An apprentice has these two objectives while the master or trainer not only gets unpaid helper but also earns some income by means of fee for imparting training and other charges which help a small-scale unit to keep on going. The apprentice in return of services provided during apprenticeship is nominally paid by the unit in accordance of his services. However, fee paid for apprenticeship and per diem paid to the apprentice are always less than the fee charged by the institution and going wage-rate respectively.

The reason for dominant apprentice ship feature of the informal sector could be explained that hired labour can not be affordable for small-size units. While bleak employment prospects and unaffordable or discontinued education induces would-be-job seekers and especially their parents to go for the acquisition of some skills with a long-term objective of establishing their own unit in future. Since a large segment of population in poor African countries can not afford education of their children due to either lack of facilities or poverty, apprenticeship for acquiring some skills leading to gainful employment in future becomes a motivating force to be in the informal sector. It requires less expenses and also no formal qualification which is necessary for getting training in the formal institutions and training centres. So the ease of entry and less expenses make them join the informal sector. Self-employment by setting up their own business is the ultimate objective of every apprentice but very few succeed due to various constraints, mainly financial.

How is the time distribution for apprentices in the informal sector of Africa may be seen from the following table:

Training Time by the Distribution of Fixed Assets

Decile/Place	*Bamako*	*Nouakchott*	*Lome*	*Yaounde*	*Kigali*
Decile I					
Training Time	7.5	7.0	6.0	6.6	N.A.
Total Working Time	50.0	51.0	49.8	53.4	32.5
Entrepreneurs Training (%)	27.3	25.0	28.0	27.8	00
Decile 2-9					
Training Time	5.8	5.2	7.2	5.6	4.0
Total Working Time	53.9	44.6	49.7	50.4	41.9
Entrepreneurs training(%)	66.4	37.3	56.1	56.7	31.8
Decile 10					
Training Time	6.2	6.5	5.2	4.5	2.0
Total Working Time	54.8	44.0	48.6	43.8	47.2
Entrepreneurs training (%)	84.2	22.2	87.5	77.8	33.3

Source : Adapted from ILO, WEP 2-33/DOC.17, Table 27, Annex.I.

(e) Unpaid Family Labour

It is a predominant characteristic of the informal sector, particularly at the micro-level. Most of the units in petty trades heavily depend on the family labour. Similarly family trades and handicrafts also have this distinct feature. Though there are no such family trades in Africa, however, handicrafts generally use family labour. Children and other family members are unpaid workers and do not receive wages. School going children in their spare time are required to provide assistance to the father and they are not paid for their work or assistance. It may have any or both the objectives *(i)* integrating children with adult work so that they get acquainted with the work or occupation for their future's sake, and *(ii)* to keep them engaged in productive economic activity at the expense of hired labour since wage employment of worker may be burdensome. Whatever, be the reason, family labour, that too unpaid is usually employed in most of the informal sector.

The ILO has listed macro-characteristics of the informal sector of Africa as : (*i*) Employment, (*ii*) Output, and (*iii*) Incomes[16].

(i) Employment

Informal sector and its concept received attention of the social scientists and recognition from the international organizations like ILO mainly on account of its employment potential. It has been presumed that the informal sector is the main provider of employment in a developing country, also in African continent, and absorbs surplus labour of the formal and other sectors of the economy. It is estimated that the informal sector of Africa absorbs three-fifth i.e. 60% of the total urban labour force. The Jobs And Skills Programme for Africa provides following employment figures for selected African countries which almost conform the estimates cited above.

The mean value comes to around 53 percent, in close proximity of the estimate, clearly establishing the fact that the informal sector provides employment to three-fifth of the total labour force in urban sector. The rest is, it is estimated, equally divided between formal sector and unemployed. These figures are merely indicative that the informal sector is the major source of employment in the urban sector of Africa, while the rate of unemployment in the urban sector comes to 20 percent. Is it a

Informal-Sector Employment in Selected African Countries (c. mid 1970s)

Aread (Country)	*Per cent of Labour Force*
Abidjan (The Ivory Coast)	44
Nairobi (Kenya)	44
Kumasi (Ghana)	65
Urban Centres of Cong (Congo)	55
Urban Centres of Senegal (Senegal)	50
Lagos (Nigeria)	50
Urban Centres of Burkina Faso (Burkino Faso)	73
Urban Centres of Bangul (Gambia)	42
Lome (Togo)	50
Urban Centres of Benin (Benin)	95
Brazzaville (Congo)	37
Urban Centres of Niger (Niger)	65
Djibouti (Djibouti)	20
Rwanda (Rwanda)	54
Lusaka (Zambia)	50
Mean- Value	52.93

Source: JASPA/ILO, Addis Ababa, 1984.

significant employment rate in the countries of Africa? To assess it, the break-up of total labour force is required. It is estimated that urban labour is only 10 to 20 percent of the total labour force in African countries. If so then employment of the three-fifth of only 10 or 20 percent of the total labour force is not significant in any way. Hence, the informal sector of Africa should not be considered as a substantial provider of employment. More-over diverse nature of African countries must be taken into careful consideration before jumping at any conclusion. In most of the west African countries informal sector dominates the urban economy while in the east African countries informal sector is emerging. Similarly, southern African countries have negligible informal sector. So a cautious approach towards drawing conclusion is recommended.

A myth is also broken that the informal sector, which is largely urban based, has a lot of employment potential. The figures speak a different language as in the African countries this sector has accommodated only three-fifth of 10 to 20 percent of total labour force. A hypothetical example may drive home the point raised here. Suppose X country has a total labour force of

1000 where the urban labour force is only 10 percent of it, that is, 100. The informal sector absorbs only 3/5 x 100 give employment figure of 60. It means that only 60 out of 1000 are employed by the informal sector which is, in terms of percentage, 6% only. It by no mean, is a substantial contribution. The same kind of situation exists in many African countries where the informal sector, typically urban-based, employs a fraction of total labour force. While the agricultural sector still has the largest employment and as compared to it, informal sector comes no where near to it.

(b) Output

The output in the informal sector of Africa has been 'guesstimated' around 20 percent of total urban output[17]. If this contribution of the informal sector, i.e, one-fifth of the total urban output is spread over three-fifth of the total urban labour force then one can guess the average contribution of workers employed in the informal sector.

It is true that some sub-sectors are contributing significantly in the informal sector vis-à-vis formal sector, for example, its contribution in woodwork is 29 percent in Lome, in building trade it is 28 percent. But this sort of disaggregated picture misleads about the contribution of the informal sector. When total contribution of the informal sector vis-à-vis formal sector is computed or 'guesstimated', it may tell an altogether story. Hence, highlighting of such sub-sectoral contributions of the informal sector should be taken in an extremely cautious manner, especially in the case of the African countries. The employment potential of the informal sector of Africa seems *priori* different from that of Asia.

(c) Incomes

The operators in the informal sector may be, following the JASPA, categorized into *(i)* masters or trainers, *(ii)* skilled workers, *(iii)* unskilled workers, and *(iv)* apprentices. Its natural that the income levels of these categories would be different from each other but it is not an issue here. The question is: do the workers failling in these categories earn income less or more than the legal minimum wages? In other words, do the worker of a particular category in the informal sector gets wages equal to the worker of the same category working in the formal sector? It is generally presumed and also observed that the wages in the formal sector are in accordance of the laws and not violate the legal minimum wages. JASPA provides the following table in this regard:

Informal-Sector Workers Earning Less than the Legal Minimum Wage

(Percentages)

Category/Place	*Bamako*	*Nauakchott*	*Lome*	*Yaounde*	*Kigali*
Masters	7.0	8.5	15.5	2.8	6.9
Skilled Workers	13.2	7.8	32.9	1.8	22.5
Unskilled Workers	43.1	54.2	100.0	66.7	0.0
Apprentices	92.8	96.0	99.3	100.0	92.9

Source: Adopted from ILO, WEP 2-33/Doc. 17, Table 9.

As may be seen from the table these are apprentices who are not paid the legal minimum wage in any country. This is true for almost all the countries in Africa. Then comes the category of unskilled workers, except Kigali, who in a large percentage get less than the minimum wage. This exploitation even reaches 100 percent in Lome. A small percentage of skilled workers, ranging between 1.8 and 32.9 is denied minimum wage-rate while masters, category shows less discrimination as a very small percentage is paid less than the minimum wages. It is evident that 'working poor' of the informal sector is apprentice category. What is the reason for discrimination against unskilled workers and apprentices? One of the obvious reason is the large supply of unskilled workers and apprentices. How it becomes possible not to pay minimum wage-rate prescribed legally? It is because the sector is not only unregulated but neglected by most of governments in developing countries. Till the informal sector gets proper recognition from governments, violation of legal wage-rate shall continue.

(d) Capital-Output Ratio

It should be another important macro-characteristic of the informal sector in any developing country but has been completely ignored by JASPA in its approach[18] towards the informal sector in Africa. Theoretically, it is safely presumed that the capital-output ratio should be high in the informal sector in comparison of the formal sector. Analogously labour-output ratio is also high in the informal sector vis-à-vis formal sector in Africa. The logic to explain the phenomena may be that the informal sector uses whatever capital, its output is generally low mainly due to technological and economies of scale reasons. Hence, per unit of output, capital units would be relatively high comparing with that of the formal sector. Similarly, formal sector uses labour-saving devices which gives less labour-output ratio than that of the informal sector. Theoretically and in simplicity all this seems sound, however, empirical evidences are warranted. The phenomenon of the 'low-level production' in the informal sector's units, widely recognized, may provide evidence of its higher 'capital-output' and 'labour-output' ratios, *if empirically tested.*

The informal sector in African countries has been important in the urban economy in two ways. Firstly, by providing employment to the tune of three-fifth of the total urban labour force. Secondly, it contributes one-fifth of total urban output in African countries. However, its role regarding employment potential should not be exaggerated as it has a limited employment potential and, at present, has no potential of growing at such a rate to absorb rising urban population due to natural and socio-economic factors. Moreover, situation differs even between, e.g. Africa and Francophone Africa.

FACTORS INDUCING CHILD LABOUR

A number of factors induce child labour directly or indirectly in the African countries. Poverty is the one factor which directly induces child labour. African countries are generally at, or near the bottom of their Human Development Index developed by the UNDP[19]. Thus the poverty leads children to work. Since socio-cultural milieu in African society is such that children start working at an early stage, say, seven year onwards. The contributing factors which eventually force a child to work are rising cost of living, growing unemployment and dwindling incomes of the workers, that is further perpetuation of poverty. The ranking as well as HDI of African countries, indicative of poverty, are given below:

Human Development Index of African Countries

Country	*HDI*	*Country Rank*
I- Eastern Africa:		
Ethiopia	0.173	138
Kenya	0.366	114
Madagascar	0.325	115
Mauritius	0.793	48
Somalia	0.088	151
Sudan	0.157	145
Tanzania	0.268	126
Uganda	0.192	133
Southern Africa:		
Botswana	0.534	94
Lesotho	0.423	107
Malawi	0.166	141
Mozamibique	0.153	146
Namibia	0.295	122
Zambia	0.315	117
Zimbabwe	0.397	108
Central Africa:		
Angola	0.169	139
Burundi	0.165	142
Cameroon	0.313	118
Central African Republic	0.159	144
Chad	0.088	150
Congo	0.372	113
Gabon	0.545	91
Rwanda	0.186	134
Zaire	0.262	127
Western Africa:		
Benin	0.111	149
Burkina Faso	0.074	157
Cote d' Ivoire	0.289	123
Ghana	0.310	119
Guinea	0.052	160
Guinea-Bissau	0.088	152

Country	*HDI*	*Country Rank*
Liberia	0.227	131
Mali	0.081	155
Mauritania	0.141	148
Niger	0.078	156
Nigeria	0.241	128
Senegal	0.178	136
Sierra Leone	0.062	159
Togo	0.218	132
Northern Africa:		
Algeria	0.533	95
Egypt	0.385	110
Libydn Arab Jamahiriya	0.659	74
Morocco	0.429	106
Tunisia	0.582	87

Source: Adapted from UNDP (1992), *World Report on Human Development*, Paris, Economica.

All the African countries may be grouped according to their HDI in the following manner:

Out of 43 countries, 37, that is, 86 percent countries have HDI less than 0.5 while only six countries have HDI more than 0.5 but less than 0.8. Since the Human Development Index which is an indicator of poverty point it out that most of African countries are poorest and hence, child labour is bound to be there in a substantial manner. Though there is no direct link between HDI and child labour, however, HDI may be taken as symptom of the child labour.

Other factor indirectly inducing children being put to work are external indebtedness[20] of the African countries. The external debt of a country adversely affects certain budgetary allocations like education, health and welfare provisions. Thus children are affected due to cuts in budget allocation on these items. For example, education facilities and child work have a sort of inverse relationship—more are education facilities, less children are drifted to work (see the figure). Conversely, scarce schooling facilities put more children to work. Compulsory primary schooling, for example is the most important instrument for arresting child labour till the age of twelve. Since education is a

Grouping of African Countries

HDI of African Countries

<0.1	*>0.1 & <0.2*	*>0.2 & <0.3*	*>0.3 & <0.4*	*>0.4 & <0.5*	*>0.5 & <0.6*	*>0.6 & <0.7*	*>0.7 & <0.8*
Somalia, Chad, Burkino-Faso, Guinea, Guinea-Bissau, Mali, Niger, Sierra-Leone	Ethiopia, Sudan, Uganda, Malawi, Mozambique, Angola, Burundi, Central African Rep., Benin, Rwanda, Mauritania, Senegal	Tanzania, Namibia, Zaire, Cote d' Ivoire, Liberia, Nigeria, Togo.	Kenya, Madagascar, Zambia, Zimbabwe, Cameroon, Congo, Ghana, Egypt	Lesotho, Morocco.	Botswana, Gabon, Algeria, Tunisia.	Libyan Arab Jamahiriya	Mauritius

social right hence primary education be expanded in the social sector, especially in the countries of Asia and Africa. It would also prevent child labour at early age. On the contrary, when the government curtails its budgetary allocation due to, the so-called, austerity measure which has become a part and parcel of funding by international institutions, to narrow deficit, education facilities also get affected in an adverse manner. Consequently, education becomes expensive and beyond the reach of poor parents who, in turn, withdraw their children from schools and put them to work. Therefore, insufficient education facilities and rising cost of education induce parents of poor income groups to put their children to work and not to schooling.

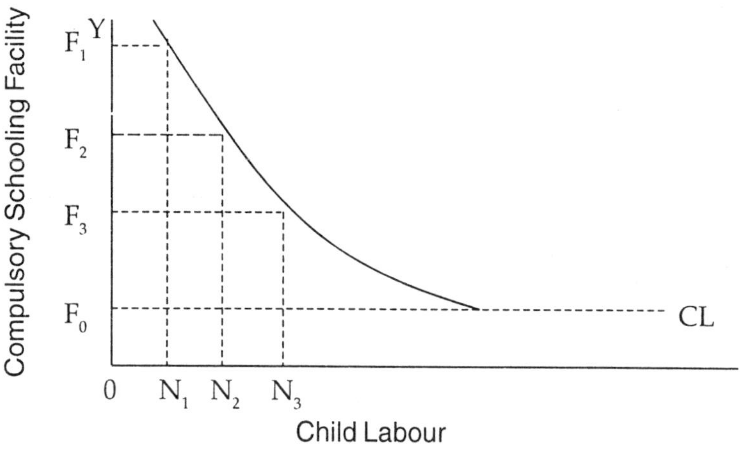

FIGURE 5.1 : *Relationship between Child Labour and Compulsory Schooling*

Globalization in recent years has warranted structural adjustment in all the economies including those in African countries. However, structural adjustments cause austerity in public and social sector. Growing poverty and income inequalities get reflected in "reduced government funding for public education programmes, lower personal incomes and family budgets available for education, and an increased focus on encouraging private education initiatives, which only some can afford".[21] Hence, structural adjustment through reduced government funding induces child labour. Studies[22] focusing on child labour are critical of structural adjustment because of its relation[23] with education.

Child labour in the rural areas of Africa may be divided into three categories viz. (*i*) domestic chores, (*ii*) farm work, and (*iii*) rural informal sector work[24]. In the early stage children start work while assisting in domestic chores. The second stage, that is, beyond seven and twelve year they work on farms and also in the rural informal sector, e.g. crafts and shopkeeping. Since the informal sector in its entirety, conducive to working children due to its characteristics child labour is largely used after agricultural sector in Africa.

References

1. Challis, J. & D. Elliman (1979), *Child Workers Today,* Middlesex (U.K.), Quarter maine House Ltd., *Chapter VII : Africa & the Middle East,* p. 91.
2. U.S. Deptt. of Labour (1994), *By the Sweat & Toil of Children*, Washington D.C., Bureau of International Labour Affairs, p. 6.
3. Morice, A. (1981), "The Exploitation of Children in the 'Informal Sector': Proposals for Research", in G. Rodgers & G. Standing (eds.), *Child Work, Poverty and Underdevelopment,* Geneva, ILO. p. 132.
4. Bekombo, M. (1981), "The Child in Africa : Socialization, Education and Work", in Rodgers & G. Standing, *op. cit.*, p. 117.
5. *Ibid*, p. 119.
6. Challis, J & D., Elliman (1979), *op. cit.*, p. 91.
7. *Ibid*, p. 93.
8. Torry, W. (1973), *Subsistence Ecology among the Gabra: Nomads of the Kenya, Ethopia Frontier, Ph.D. Dissertaion*, Columbia University, (Mimeo), pp. 156-62.
9. Kane, A.S. (1995), "The Work of Child Nomads" , in J. Ennew (ed.), *Learning or Labouring*?, Florence, ICDC (UNICEF), p. 68.
10. *Ibid*, p. 69.
11. Challis, J. & D. Elliman (1979), *op. cit.*, p. 97.
12. JASPA (1986), *The Challenge of Employment & Basic Needs in Africa*, Nairobi, Oxford University Press, pp 249-53.
13. *Ibid*, p. 250.
14. *Ibid*.
15. *Ibid*, p. 252.
16. *Ibid*, pp. 245-49.
17. JASPA (1986), *op. cit.*, p. 247.
18. JASPA (1986), "The informal Sector in Africa", in JASPA/ILO (ed), *op. cit.*, pp. 244-60.

19. UNDP (1992), *World Report on Human Development*, Paris, Economica.
20. ILO (1992), *Child Labour in Tanzania,* Geneva, ILO, pp. 16-17.
21. Reimers, F. & L. Tiburcio, (1993), *Education, Adjustment and Reconstruction Options for Change*, Paris, UNESCO, p. 14.
22. ILO (1992), Towards *Action Against Child Labour in Zimbabwe*, Geneva, ILO, pp. 53-54.
23. Carnoy, M. (1995), "Structural Adjustment and the Changing Face of Education", *International Labour Review*, vol. 134: 6, pp. 653-73.
24. Bonnet, M. (1993), "Child Labour in Africa", *International Labour Review,* vol. 132: 3, pp. 382.

7. CHILD LABOUR HAZARDS

Child labour is, in itself, a hazard. However, hazardous work in the language of the ILO[1] may be described in the following manner:

(*a*) "Work which exposes children to physical, emotional or sexual abuse;

(*b*) Work underground, under water, at dangerous heights or in confined spaces;

(*c*) Work with dangerous machinery, equipment and tools, or which involves the manual handling or transport of heavy loads;

(*d*) Work in an unhealthy environment which may, for example, expose children to hazardous substances, agents or processes, or to temperatures, noise levels, or vibrations damaging to their health;

(*e*) Work under particularly difficult conditions such as work for long hours or during the night or work which does not allow for the possibility of returning home each day."

The obvious reasons are: child workers are not physically and mentally developed like adults and hence, liable to misjudge or misunderstand instructions related to work or job assigned. Children may not cope with heavy work and load carrying due to their low physical strength. Similarly, mental development at a young stage, say up to fifteen years of age is never high *vis-à-vis* adults. Thus child workers have mental limitations as well. These two limitations make them more vulnerable to thwart any danger or bear the brunt. But also their perception, visualization and anticipation are poor. Hence, children are more vulnerable to occupational hazards.

Another limitation which exposes them to work hazard is educational level of working children. It is either nil or very low. These are generally school drop-out and get engaged in work. Such working children have an extremely limited capacity and ability in reading, writing and numeracy. Unable to read and therefore follow instructions printed on a machine which child workers operate, expose them to hazards.

Similarly child especially female workers like maids, helpers and assistants face dangers of being molested, sexually exploited and or misguided. They get spoiled by the lure of money and fall prey very easily at a tender age.

Various types of hazards can be classified as per their nature, extent and severity in a number of ways. However, the following classification serves the purpose of exposing hazards inherent in child labour.

All important hazards for child workers have been classified into four: *(1)* Physical hazards, *(2)* Psychological hazards, *(3)* Psycho-social work hazards, and *(4)* industry/occupation related hazards. Another classifica-tion may be as endogenous hazards and exogenous hazards. However, the first-classi-fication is more eleborate and thus preferred over other. Various types of hazards are not self-explanatory and therefore need elaboration, which may easily form the subject matter for immediate elimination of the worst forms of child labour emphasized by the ILO (ILO, 1999) and other agencies.

The first type of hazards, that is, physical hazards are easily visible and seen. These are: (*i*) work place hazards, (*ii*) bodily hazards, (*iii*) health hazards, and worst of all, (*iv*) sexual hazards. Work place hazards are so common and frequent that these are not being taken very seriously except by the NGOs. Children working at dingy and dark place without proper ventilation or sanitation may be observed in every developing country having handicraft or traditional industry worth its name. Carpet industry is the most infamous in many Third World countries like Nepal, India, Pakistan, Egypt, Yemen and the list could be very long. Sub-contracting has made the situation worst as the workplaces at the periphery are usually invisible and lack all those facilities which should essentially be provided. Match-making and gem-polishing industries fall in the same category which lack basic facilities at work place. The local cigarettes industries commonly known as *bedees* in the Indian sub-continent, which is quite large and widely spread, may be another classic example of non-existent facilities at work place.

Children working in the domestic sector as maids, cleaners and helpers are being denied basic facilities in the houses where they work. All maids are usually provided food not consumed by the family of employers, used clothes and sleep either in the kitchen or some corner of the house. Those maids which stay with employer's family are more valunerable as they are supposed to attend every beck and call of every member of the family for twenty four hours a day, seven days a week and thirty days of a month. They don't have any privacy at their work place, that is the house where they work. And their belongings are always subject to inspection by any and every member of the employer's family. This particular class of child workers has more harsh working conditions and have to bear more physical hazards than any other category of working children.

The second type, i.e. body hazards are always there in the case of working children whether doing job in a house or a factory. Children have to sit in very unnatural or awkward postures for doing their work and if they continue for long, deformity is developed. For example, children working at looms for ten to sixteen hours a day, develop deformities such as hunch on their back or bending-legs etc. as their awkward posture warrants it. Similarly, continuous strain on their eyes while knotting and also due to insufficient and improper light, impairs their vision. Those children who work at noisy places like repairing shops, workshops and scrap dealers, commonly suffer from one or the other kind of hearing- impairments.

In the units of informal sector, protective measures are almost non-existent. Glass industry in Firozabad, India provides a classic example where children have to bear thermal stress while working near the open furnace having a temperature of

Child Labour Hazards

- Physical hazards
  - Work place hazards
  - Body-hazards
  - Health hazards
- Psychological hazards
  - Withdrawal
  - Strain & Stress
  - dullness
  - general apathy
  - fear
  - inferiority
  - complex
- Psycho-social work hazards
  - Stunting
  - Mental dev. slow down
  - Insecurity
  - No stimulation
- Industrial occupation related hazards
  - exposures
  - radiation, chemical toxic & non-toxic
  - thermal stress
  - others

1400 to 1600^{0} Celsius. The heat and fumes of molten glass and silica generates unbearable temperature for workers in these shady factories. Children get burns and cuts without any proper medication facilities. Such incidents are frequent and taken as work hazards, something not serious. It is a common sight in the construction industry that children carry heavy load of bricks or mud over their head. Such children working for long years get deformity in their body. Their body bears a lot of strain and they even get one or the other kind of body damage. Similarly, in brick-kilns, children have to sit-squat throughout the day which affects their body shape and growth.

Injuries are very common in almost all the jobs which children do. In mining, physical injuries are order of the day as child workers are usually not provided protective gears and safety rules are generally flouted. African mining sector is infamous for such practices and also for child workers. Another profession known for lethal accidents and injuries is deep-sea diving. The practice of *muro-ami* in The Philippines and other similar practices in Thailand, Indonesia and other countries are the best example of serious physical injuries, sometimes even lethal.

Fatigue is a common problem of child workers as they have to work for longer hours in most of occupations while their endurance to bear physical pressure is not as developed as of adults. Even in workshops and other work places, children have to do all the leg work without any laxity or consideration of their age. They get physical punishment, sometimes brutal, leaving a scar on their body for the life, for mistakes or not carrying out order of their seniors or employers. Child workers are not given proper rest period and asked to do all kinds of errands or odd jobs leading to extreme fatigue. In metal, wood and motor workshops, child workers are first to come in the morning and the last to leave in the evening, hence their working hours stretch to twelve hours. Often child workers are denied weekly off-day. It all leads to extreme fatigue and they get so exhausted that ageing becomes distinct and visible.

The violence at work place also affects young child workers. Some times they suffer at the hands of their older colleagues who beat them up. Such incidents, though not frequent, may be seen in motor garages, metal workshops, road-side tea shops and other eating places.

The health hazards are numerous and prevalent not only in the informal, household but also in agricultural sectors. Small-scale and cottage industries using chemicals such as dyes etc. pose danger for working children exposed to such dangers without any protective gears and safety measures. All the dying and printing and Kite-thread making units easily fit into the category. Child workers in such occupations commonly suffer from skin diseases.

In brassware industry of Moradabad and glass industry of Firozabad, child workers develop T.B. and other respiratory problems due to exposure to excessive heat, fumes, dust and temperatures. Respiratory problems are also common in the carpet weaving industry where child workers inhale particles of wool fluff and dust (Nangia, 1991).

There is a special category of child workers, i.e. ragpickers who are exposed not only to vagaries of weather but also to all sorts of pollutants and health risks. Those ragpicks who generally search for and collect medical wastes incur more health hazards. Infected syringes, gloves and glucose bottles etc. make the collectors more vulnerable to infectious deseases. Even contacting HIV may not be ruled out. Garbage collectors also expose themselves to various deseases due to their exposure to all sorts of pathogenes and insects breeding at their 'work places', i.e. garbage heaps.

Sexual hazards are nothing but sexual abuse and exploitation of child workers. In this category fall domestic helpers, maids in the bar and restaurants and farm workers. It is relatively more in the case of female child workers and thus has gender bias.

List of Occupations & Industries and related Hazards

Occupation/Industry	*Hazards*
1. Abattoirs & Meat rendering	injuries from cuts, burns, falls, dangerous equipments, exposure to infectious disease, heat stress.

Occupation/Industry	*Hazards*
2. Acids (work with)	risk of burns, inhalation of toxic fumes, eye injuries.
3. Agriculture	unsafe machinery, hazardous substances, accidents, chemical poisoning, arduous work, dangerous animals, insects & reptiles.
4. Alcohol	intoxication, addiction, prejudicial to morals environment, risk of violence.
5. Carpet Weaving	dust inhalation, poor lighting, poor posture (squatting), respiratory & musculo-skeletal disease, eye strain, chemical-poisoning.
6. Cement	harmful chemicals, exposure to harmful dust, arduous work, respiratory & musculo-skeletal disease.
7. Circular Saws & other dangerous machines	accidents, e.g. loss of limb or life, danger from unprotected moving parts.
8. Construction	exposure to heat, cold, dust, falling objects, accidents, musculo-skeletal diseases.
9. Cranes/hoists/lifting machinery	accidents, falling objects, musculo-skeletal disease, risk of injury to others.
10. Glass Manufacture	molten glass, extreme heat, poor ventilation, cuts from broken glass, carrying hot glass, burns, respiratory disease, heat stress, toxic dust.
11. Domestic Service	long hours, physical, emotional, sexual abuse, malnutrition, insufficient rest, isolation.
12. Electricity	dangerous work with high voltage, risk of falling, high level of responsibility for safety of others.
13. Entertainment [night clubs, bars, Casinos, circuses etc.]	long, late hours, sexual abuse, exploitation, prejudicial to morals.
14. Explosives (manufacture & handling)	risk of explosion, fire, burns, mortal danger.
15. Fumes, dust, gas & other noxious substances	chemical poisoning, damage to eyes, damage to respiratory system, poisoning.

Occupation/Industry	Hazards
16. Hospitals & diagnostic labs etc.	infectious disease, responsibility for well-being of others.
17. Lead/Zinc metallurgy, white lead, lead in paint	cumulative poisoning, neurological damage.
18. Machinery in motion (operation, cleaning, repairs etc.)	danger from moving engine parts, accidents, cuts, burns, exposure to heat & noise, noise stress, eye & ear injuries.
19. Maritime work (trimmers, stokers & stevedoring)	arduous work, musculo-skeletal disease, respiratory disease.
20. Mining, Quarries, underground work	exposure to dust, gases, fumes, dirty conditions, respiratory & musculo-skeletal disease, accidents, falling objects, arduous work, heavy loads.
21. Radio active substances or ionizing radiation (with work)	Radiation.
22. Rubber	heat, burns, chemical poisoning.
23. Street Trades	exposure to drugs, violence, criminal activities, heavy loads, musculo-skeletal diseases, veneral diseases, accidents.
24. Tanneries	chemical poisoning, sharp instruments, respiratory disease.
25. Tar, asphalt, bitumen	exposure to heat, burns, chemical poisoning, respiratory diseases.
26. Transportation, Operating vehicles	accidents, danger to self & passengers.
27. Under water	decompression illness, dangerous fish, death or injury.
28. Weights & loads	physical stress & strain, musculo-skeletal diseases.
29. Welding & Smelting of metals, metal working	exposure to extreme heat, flying sparks & hot metal objects, accidents, eye injuries, heat stress.

Source: ILO, *Conditions of Work Digest, vol. 10,* 1/1991, *Part II, Annexure* 3.

Sexual hazards do not totally exclude male child workers, especially the young ones. However, a number of countries like Nepal, India, the Philippines, Sri Lanka and Thailand may be cited as examples of sexual exploitation of young girls generally lured for employment in cities. Those in captivity suffer the most and eventually land up in the brothels.

Sex workers also undergo sexual abuse, though it seems strange. They negotiate for normal sexual intercourse but often landup in a mess when their customer compel them for unnatural sexual activities. Some inflict pain and get more pleasure which girls especially young ones have to endure. Sexual abuse of male children is on rise and several countries particularly Nordic have framed laws against it, even committed outside the country. Such legal provisions may also be taken as testimony that sexual abuse of children, male and female both has been rising. Thailand, the Philippines (Rialp, 1993), Sri Lanka and even some African countries like Kenya are being noticed as centres where sexual abuse of children, especially by the tourists has been significant. Sex workers get STD and now the danger of HIV infection and AIDS is looming large in every country.

Another category of hazards is that of psychological hazards. Child workers are relatively more susceptible to this type of hazards than the adult workers due to their tender biological age and level of mental development. Such hazards may be discussed in terms of feelings such as fear, lack of confidence, depression, inferiority complex, apathetic attitude in general, withdrawal, strain and stress and dullness. The inference is that every child worker faces one or the other of these hazards in every occupation. It varies from child to child and occupation to occupation.

Very young children suffer from the feeling of fear while learning a trade or skill and or working somewhere. They feel that damage may be done by them due to lack of experience. Those working in the household do damage or break, say crockery and utensils and fear of punishment gets instilled. A constant feeling of fear of some mistake or punishment makes them a nervous creature. It often becomes a part of their personality, as may be observed in motor garages etc. where strictness is the rule of the day. Most of child workers under ten or twelve develop fear syndrome due to one or the other reason.

Young children when forced to work also have inferiority complex as they observe other children attending school rather than doing work like them. They get this impression and feeling that we belong to lower strata of the society, called as poor. Hence, fear and inferiority complex may lead to lack of confidence in such children.

It has been observed that working children marginalized in the society, mainly due to the nature of their work, e.g. ragpickers, develop a sort of apathy towards relations and society as a whole. Rosario's study (Rosario, 1988) on child ragpickers and their behaviour highlights this characteristic as well. The ragpickers due to apathetic attitude of the society, develop withdrawal symptom and eventually have apathy for the society and their emotional relations.

Fear, complex, apathetic attitude and withdrawal may lead to depression in the working children. This is true particularly for those children who are maltreated and physically abused. Children in 'captivity' known as bonded labourers generally confine their emotions and feelings to themselves and are bound to suffer from depression. Children away from their homes and confined to workplace, say carpet weavers in Mirzapur (India) who are kept isolated from the society by their employers or contractors, have been found depressed. The reasons for their depression are multiple, such as, loneliness, long working hours at a dingy and semi-dark places, no freedom to move out, no visitors from the family or home, lack of facilities, punishments, sometimes physical abuse from the older fellow etc. These and such other factors cause depression, surely in the long run.

Another psycho-problem generally faced by child workers is dullness. Those working children who do repetitive work day after day become quite dull. Children working in metal, wood and or motor workshops do the same kind of job every day which becomes quite boring. When they go on repeating the same work day after day and month after month, dullness in their behaviour, personality and functioning assumes a distinctive feature. Thus the psychological hazards affect not only mental but physical health as well.

Psycho-social work hazards lead to stunting, slow down mental development, cause the feeling of insecurity and provide no stimulation for work among child workers. The psychological and social aspects of work may be hazards for working children if work-conditions and nature are not healthy.

Children are usually employed or engaged as trainees, apprentices, helpers and to do errands. In family business or occupation, children feel secure and worthy as they get affection and appreciation from their family members. On the contrary, as employees they have the lowest status which makes them not-so-comfortable at their work place. If treatment is harsh, their inability to defend or retaliate gives them a feeling of vulnerability. They are always at the mercy of their employers, who have total authority makes them realize their weak position and no recourse to any compensation or relief mechanism. Insecurity crops up when there is no recourse for working children as they can not be a member of any trade union or no organization exists for their rights. Mostly work places are devoid of basic facilities. Children, for example, work in awkward postures in carpet, glass and match-making factories which result in stunting their physical growth. They don't have spontaneous and open social interaction with other children necessary for their mental and physical growth. It all leads to no-stimulation-situation, deterimental to mental and physical growth and personality development of child workers. Such psycho-social work hazards are common in occupations generally open to child workers, especially in the Third World countries.

The most obvious hazards are occupational or industrial. These are prevalent in almost every developing country engaging a large force of child labour. Though a number of countries have identified occupations/ industries hazardous for child workers, informal sector has escaped from the laws banning child labour in hazardous occupations and industrial units or establishment. The following table excerpted from ILO(ILO, 1991) and quoted in Bequele and Myers (Bequele & Myers, 1995) gives a general picture of occupations/industries considered hazardous for child workers of different age in different countries.

Occupation/ Industry	Hazards	Min. age (in years)	Country
Abattoirs & meat rendering	Injuries from cuts, burns, falls, dangerous equipments, exposure to infectious disease, heat stress	18	Central African Republic, Congo, Gabon, Finland, Luxembourg, Togo, U.S.A., Zaire
		16	Bahrain, Lebanon
Acids (work with)	Risk of burns, inhalation of toxic fumes, eye injuries	18	Angola, Austria, Bolivia, Cameroon, Chad, Colombia, Congo, Cyprus, Denmark, France, Germany, Spain, Sudan, Togo
		16	Bharain, Honduras, Mexico
Agriculture	Unsafe machinery, hazardous substances, accidents, chemical poisoning, arduous work, dangerous animals, insects & reptiles	21	Uruguay
		18	Colombia, Costa Rica, Spain
		17	Australia (Queensland)
		16 or 18	France
		16	Denmark, U.K., U.S.A.
Alcohol Production and/or sale	Intoxication, addiction, environment prejudicial to moral, risk of violence	21	Chile
		18	Argentina, Australia (Victoria), Bolivia, Brazil, Burundi, Cameroon, Colombia, Costa Rica, Dominican Republic, Ecuador, Equatorial Guinea, Haiti, Italy, Luxembourg, Mexico, Panama, Peru, Portugal, Spain, Swaziland, Venezuela, Zaire
		16	Gautemala, Honduras, Mexico
		15	Jamaica, Thailand
Carpet-Weaving	Dust inhalation, poor lighting, poor posture, respiratory	14	India

Occupation/ Industry	Hazards	Min. age (in years)	Country
	musculo-skeletal disease, eye strain, chemical poisoning		
Cement	Harmful chemicals, exposure to harmful dust, arduous work, respiratory & musculo-skeletal disease	18	Angola, Cameroon, Colombia
		14	India
Circular Saws & other dangerous machines	Accidents	18	Argentina, Australia (Victoria), Austria, Bolivia, Cameroon, Colombia, Denmark, Djibouti, Ecuador, France, Gabon, India, Luxembourg, Madagascar, Mauritius, Nepal, Peru, S. Arabia, Spain, Trinidad & Tobago, U.S.A., Zaire
		17	Pakistan
		16	Burkina Faso, Chad, Central African Republic, Congo, Malaysia, Senegal, U.K.
Construction and/or demolition	Exposure to heat, cold, dust, falling objects, accidents, musculo-skeletal diseases	18	Austria, Bolivia, Burundi, Colombia, El-Salvador, France, Gabon, Luxembourg, Madagascar, Netherlands, Peru, Spain, U.S.A.
		16	Bahrain, Barbados, Burkina Faso, Cameroon, Central African Republic, Chad, Congo, Cote d'Ivoire, Djibouti, France, Kenya,

Occupation/ Industry	Hazards	Min. age (in years)	Country
			Morocco, Senegal, Somalia, U.K.
		15	Dominica, Jamaica
		14	Belize, Cyprus, India
Cranes/hoists/ lifting machinery	Accidents, falling objects, musculo-skeletal disease, risk of injury to others	18	Argentina, Austria, Canada, Central African Republic, Chad, Colombia, Congo, Gabon, Japan, Luxembourg, Madagascar, Mauritius Netherlands, U.S.A., Zaire
		16	Bahrain, Denmark, France, Israel
Crystal and/or Glass Manufacture	Molten glass, extreme heat, poor ventilation, cuts from broken glass, carrying hot glass, burns, respiratory disease, heat stress, toxic dust	18	Angola, Argentina, Austria, Bolivia, Cameroon, Cote d'-Ivoire, Colombia, Cyprus (women), Denmark, Djibouti, Ecuador, Ireland, Madagascar, Senegal
		17	Austria
		16-18	France
		16	Bahrain
		15	Syrian Arab Republic
Domestic	Long hours, physical, emotional, sexual abuse, malnutrition, insufficient rest, isolation	16	Denmark
Electricity	Dangerous work with high voltage, risk of falling, high level of responsibility for safety of others	18	Angola, Cameroon, Colombia, France, Panama, Sweden, Uruguay, Zaire
		16	Bahrain, Mexico Dominica, Jamaica
		14	Belize

Occupation/ Industry	Hazards	Min. age (in years)	Country
Entertainment [night clubs, bars, Casinos, circuses, gambling halls]	Long, late hours, sexual abuse, exploitation, prejudicial to morals	21	Chile, Seychelles (Casinos), Uruguay
		18	Angola, Austria, Bolivia, Brazil, Burundi, Cameroon, Colombia, Ecuador, El Salvador, Italy, Luxembourg, Panama, Peru, Philippines Seychelles, Switzerland
		16	France, Honduras
		15	Thailand
Explosives (mfr. & handling)	Risk of explosion, fire, burns, mortal danger	18	Angola, Austria, Bolivia, Belgium, Burundi, Cameroon, Chad, Colombia, Congo, Costa-Rica, Cote d' Ivoire, Cyprus, Denmark, Djibouti, Ecuador, El-Salvador, Equatorial-Guinea, Finland, France, Japan, Lao People's Democratic Republic, Luxembourg, Madagascar, Netherlands, Panama, Peru, Philippines, Portugal, Senegal, Spain, Sweden, Switzerland, Thailand, Togo, U.S.A, Zaire
		17	Canada (Federal)
		16	Bahrain, Dominican Republic, Honduras, Mexico, Morocco
		14	India
Fumes, dust, gas & other noxious substances	Chemical poisoning, damage to eyes, damage to respiratory system,	18	Angola, Austria, Bolivia, Congo, Czech Republic, Denmark, Ecuador, El-Salvador, France,

Occupation/ Industry	Hazards	Min. age (in years)	Country
	poisoning		Germany, Japan, Lao-PDR, Luxembourg, Madagascar, Netherlands, Nicaragua, Peru, Portugal, Slovakia, Spain, Sudan, Sweden, Switzerland, Thailand, Togo
		17	Cuba
		16	Bahrain, Honduras, Mexico, Morocco, U.K.
		14	India
Hospitals & work with risk of infection	Infectious diseases, responsibility for well-being of others	18	Austria, Bangladesh, Czech Republic, Luxembourg, Madagascar, Netherlands, Slovakia, Spain, Switzerland
		17	Israel
Lead/Zinc metallurgy white lead, lead in paint	Cumulative poisoning, neurological damage	21	Uruguay
		18	Australia (Queensland, Victoria), Austria, Barbados, Belgium, Bolivia, Cameroon, Colombia, Cyprus, Czech Republic, Denmark, Djibouti, Ecuador, France, Gabon, Germany, Ireland, Madagascar, Malta, Norway, Slovakia, Sudan, Sweden, Syrian Arab Republic, Togo, Zaire
		16	Bahrain, Greece, Honduras, Mexico, U.K.
		15	Syrian Arab Republic
Machinery in motion (operation, cleaning, repairs etc.)	Danger from moving engine parts, accidents, cuts, burns,	21	Uruguay
		18	Argentina, Austria, Bolivia, Burundi, Cameroon, Central

Occupation/ Industry	Hazards	Min. age (in years)	Country
	exposure to heat & noise, noise stress, eye & ear injuries		African Republic, Colombia, Chad, Congo, Cote d' Ivoire, Cyprus, Denmark, Djibouti, Dominica, Dominican Republic, El-Salvador, Equatorial Guinea, France, Gabon, Greece, India, Ireland, Japan, Luxembourg, Madagascar, Malawi, Malta, Mauritius, Myanmar, Netherlands, Peru, S. Arabia, Spain, Sweden, Switzerland, Thailand, Zaire, Zambia
		17	Pakistan
		16	Bahrain, Bangladesh, Djibouti, Guyana, Jamaica, Malaysia, Morocco, Nigeria, Saint Lucia, Senegal, Singapore, U.K.
		15	Italy, Syrian Arab Republic
Maritime work (trimmers, stokers & stevedoring)	Accidents, heat, burns, falls from heights, heavy lifting, arduous work, musculo-skeletal disease, respiratory disease	21	Brazil
		19	Denmark, Iceland
		18	Algeria, Argentina, Australia, Bahamas, Bangladesh, Belgium, Belize, Burundi, China, Congo, Cote d' Ivoire, Djibouti, Ecuador, El-Salvador, Fiji, Gabon, Iraq, Ireland, Japan, Kenya, Liberia, Luxembourg, Malawi, Malta, Myanmar, Nigeria, Pakistan, Peru, Philippines, Romania, Sierra Leone, Singapore,

Occupation/ Industry	Hazards	Min. age (in years)	Country
			Solomon Islands, Somalia, Srilanka, Sudan, Tanzania, Trinidad & Tobago, Tunisia, Yugoslavia, Zaire
		17	Canada (Federal), Cuba
Mining, Quarries, underground work	Exposure to dust, gases, fumes, dirty conditions, respiratory & musculo-skeletal diseases, accidents, falling objects, arduous work, heavy-loads	21	Brazil
		18	Afghanistan, Albania, Angola, Argentina, Australia, Austria, Belgium, Bolivia, Botswana, Burundi, Belarus, Cameroon, Cape Verde, Central African Rep., Chad, Chile, Colombia, Congo, Cuba, Cyprus, Czech-Rep., Denmark, Djibouti, Dominican Rep., Ecuador, El Salvador, Equatorial Guinea, Fiji, France, Gabon, Germany, Ghana, Greece, Guinea Bissau, India, Indonesia, Iraq, Ireland, Israel, Italy, Japan, Jordan, Lao PDR, Luxembourg, Nicaragua, Panama, Peru, Philippines, Portugal, Russian Federation, Sao-Tome & Principe, Saudi Arabia, Slovakia, Somalia, Sudan, Swaziland, Switzerland, Tanzania, Thailand, Tunisia, Turkey, U.S.A., Venezuela, Yugoslavia, Zaire, Zambia
		17	Australia (Victoria),

Occupation/ Industry	Hazards	Min. age (in years)	Country
			Bangladesh, Canada (Federal), Jamaica, Myanmar, Pakistan
		16	Bahrain, Barbados, Burkina Faso, Cote d'-Ivoire, Hungary, Kenya, Lesotho, Mexico, Nicaragua, Nigeria, Sierra Leone, Singapore, Solomon Island, U.K.
		15	Dominica, Syrian Arab Rep.
		14	Belize, Cyprus
Radio active substances or ionizing radiation (with work)	Radiation	18	Argentina, Austria, Belgium, Colombia, Czech Rep., Denmark, Finland, France, Germany, India, Lao PDR, Luxembourg, Malta, Netherlands, Panama, Philippines, Slovakia, Sudan, Thailand, U.S.A.
		17	Canada (Federal)
		16	Bahrain, Guyana, Honduras, U.K.
Rubber	Heat, burns, chemical poisoning	18	Angola, Cyprus
		16	Mexico
Street Trades	Exposure to drugs, violence, criminal activities, heavy loads, musculo-skeletal diseases, veneral diseases, accidents	18	Austria, Bolivia, Brazil
		16	Peru, Burkina Faso, Cyprus, Djibouti (women), Dominican Rep., Italy, U.K.
		15	Costa Rica
		14	Sri Lanka
Tanneries	Chemical poisoning, sharp instruments, respiratory	18	Chad, France, Gabon, Zaire
		17	Austria
		16	Dominicam Rep., Mexico

Occupation/ Industry	Hazards	Min. age (in years)	Country
	disease	15	Syrian Arab Rep.
		14	India
Tar, asphalt, bitumen	Exposure to heat, burns, chemical poisoning, respiratory diseases	18	Angola, Czech Rep., Luxembourg, Slovakia
		15	Syrian Arab Rep.
Transportation, Operating vehicles	Accidents, danger to self & passengers	18	Austria, Burundi, Central African Rep., Chad, Congo, Denmark, Equatorial Guinea, Gabon, Pakistan, Panama, Peru, Philippines, Spain, U.S.A., Zaire
		16	Barbados, Dominican Rep., Israel, Kenya, U.K.
		15	Dominica, Jamaica
		14	Belize, Cyprus
Under water	Decompression illness, dangerous fish, death or injury	18	Austria, Colombia, El-Salvador, Lao PDR, Sudan, Sweden, Thailand, Turkey
		16	Dominican Rep., Mexico
Weights & loads	Physical stress & strain, musculo-skeletal diseases	14-18	Australia (Victoria), Belgium, Belize, Bolivia, Botswana, Burkina Faso, Burundi, Cameroon, Central African Rep., Chad, Congo, Cote d'-Ivoire, Cuba, Cyprus, Czech Rep., Djibouti, Ecuador, Gabon, India, Israel, Italy, Niger, Russian Federation, Slovakia, Spain, Switzerland, Ukraine, Uruguay, Zaire

Occupation/ Industry	Hazards	Min. age (in years)	Country
Welding & Smelting of metals, metal working	Exposure to extreme heat, flying sparks & hot metal objects, accidents, eye injuries, heat stress	18	Argentina, Austria, Bolivia, Cameroon, Colombia, Ecuador, Luxembourg, Spain, Sudan, Sweden, U.S.A.
		16	Bahrain

Note: The information given in this list may not reflect completely and in detail the situation in the countries. Some countries that cover the listed hazardous occupations or industries in their minimum age legislation may not be mentioned here, in particular if coverage is provided by a general prohibition of all types of employment or work which jeopardizes the health, safety or morals of young persons.

Source: adapted from Conditions of Work Digest, vol. X, 1/1991, Part II, Annex III.

The list, given above, provides not only the names of those countries where legislation regarding hazardous work and minimum age for working children exists but also occupations and or industries which are considered hazardous. It also describes the nature of hazards associated with specific occupations and or industries. Hence, international comparison vis-à-vis minimum age of working children in hazardous occupation or industry is possible and inferences may be drawn. A word of caution. The foregoing list does not give details of legislation, hence comparison be made cautiously for further study.

Industrial and or occupational hazards have many dimensions like exposures to radiation, toxic substances and fumes, poisoning and thermal stress. Sometime such hazards lead to lethal accidents. Union Carbide's industrial hazard took a heavy toll in India and may not be forgotten for long time.

Such gas emissions, leakages, radiations and other exposures do affect adult workers. But children workers are affected more severely and seriously. A quantity of toxic substance or its fumes or gases may not be lethal for an adult but may be for a child. Hence, child workers in the brass- ware, glass, nickel plating suffer more in terms of health and diseases.

So far the hazards. The logical question is: how to protect working children from hazards? Bequele and Myers (1995, pp 29-41) have suggested two types of approaches namely, preventive and rehabilitative to protect child workers from hazards.

The preventive approach mainly focuses on reducing or eliminating the employment of children and the following way have been suggested to achieve the goal.

Firstly, economic development and better income distribution, which has been termed as 'economic development' approach, may achieve the target. Theoretically it sounds well. However, economic development, that too, accompanied with fair distribution of income has been a distant dream for the countries of the Third World. It is, as admitted, a long term process which would certainly take its heavy toll in terms of child labour during the course of time. Developing countries having inherent characteristics of income-inequality, regional disparity and resource constraints may find in *faux pass* if economic development cum equality in income distribution approach is adopted for reducing the employment of children. The approach *per se* is not deficient and or ineffective but its implementation keeping in view the socio-economic milieu in the Third World seems an uphill task.

Secondly, social security and assistance policy has been advocated for reducing the employment of children, termed as 'targeted income' approach. It is more viable and liable to be translated into action, if and only if a selective-family-targeted income approach is opted to tackle the issue. It is tantamount to say that families be selected in a phased manner for targeted income level so as to prevent child labour. Not only the most vulnerable classes but means of accruing income be identified so that children may not drift into the labour market. The efficacy of this type of policy shall depend on a number of factors like political will, good governance and substantial funding from donors and international agencies. NGOs may play a really important and effective role from identification to implementation to monitoring rather than the bureaucratic set up of the government known for its inefficiency and corruption.

Thirdly, discouragement of children from entering employment is being suggested as a preventive measure, by means of 'educational' approach. Free and compulsory education up to a certain level say 12 years, should be effective in preventing child employment. Again the crux of the problem is financial and infra-structure constraint. It is obvious and known that one of the best anti-child labour law is compulsory education but how to meet the financial requirements of such a gigantic task in a poor country? Such an ambitious scheme be thought twice prior to being implemented. But it has a lot of potential as demonstrated by, what is known as, Kerala model. Sincere and concerted efforts in this direction may really pave the way, provided there is a will and commitment.

Fourthly, is suggested the prevention of employers from hiring children. Every country signatory to the ILO convention has legislation in this regard and even then 'prevention of employers from hiring children' recommendation simply means that it is not effective in any developing country. The main culprit is informal sector hiring child labour. Hence, legalisation of informal sector is really important to regulate it, only then effective implementation of legislation would be a possibility as informal sector happens to be the main harbour of child labour.

The usually ignored sector is agriculture where child labour is generally a part of family labour. Children in an agricultural family do work on their family farms. During the sowing and harvesting periods their help is sought. They work hard and sometimes work even during nights. This aspect of child labour is mostly ignored as if it is not exploitative. Sometimes children have to work in the field rather than attending their school. There is no question of playing games or leisure. Such engagements at the cost of either schooling or leisure differentiates child work from child labour.

In developing countries like India, Nigeria, Somalia etc. children may be seen spraying pesticides and applying fertilizers which is inimical to their health. They are not taught to safeguard themselves from inhaling toxic substances. Children below eighteen years of age may be observed driving tractors and operating threshers. Accidents particularly during harvesting period are not a rarity. There is no agricultural activity in which children over 10 years are not engaged. It is considered a natural way of their upbringing in rural areas, e.g., in South Asian, South east Asian and African and Latin American countries. How to prevent children from such 'employment' and safeguard them against all those hazards? Simply by educating their parents through the available means of mass media, especially television and other visual media as majority of farmers is not educated. Such agricultural hazards are common and rising in the countries of the Third World where agriculture is not mechanized or semi-mechanised. In case of hired child labour, prevention is more difficult since employers have a casual attitude towards child workers.

The same is true in case of handicrafts, be it family occupation or employment. The craftmen start teaching their art to their children at a very tender age, particularly sons. It is believed that their sons would inherit the family tradition and thereby occupation. Its common examples are Kite thread making where children help and learn dye, use of glass particles for the thread. It damages their skin and exposes children to other health problems. Similarly, sequine work is too strenuous for children as it gives a lot of strain to their eyes. Moreover, they have to sit squatted around the frame for long hours. A posture which leads even to deformity. Such handicrafts and family occupations expose children to various hazards. Moreover, invisible work being done with in four walls of the house are not easy to be detected and checked. Even the hired child labour in such professions and trades remains invisible and hence prevention of employers from hiring children is difficult.

Another problem is that of self-employed child labour. Street vending and other such activities may be checked. But some activities for which children are compelled by their circumstances may not be easy to be prevented, though expose them to various kinds of hazards. Such an activity is ragpicking. A large number of young children, even under ten are engaged in ragpicking, notably in India, the Philippines and other developing countries. These children are usually not hired by the employers and work on their own to sell re-usable things to junk dealers. Collecting their 'chosen' articles from garbage heaps, dump-sites, waste-bins and other such extremely unhygienic place exposes them to various diseases, cuts and injuries. Those child ragpickers who collect hospital waste are prone to be the carrier of HIV as they come in the contact of syringes, gloves and other surgical or medical instruments used for HIV patients. They work with bare hands and even a scratch or ordinary wound may cause deadly infection. How about the prevention of such hazards? NGOs have been playing some role but such efforts are not sufficient from the view point of prevention. It needs more thinking, more efforts and feasible policy measures.

Another approach termed 'technological development' approach as preventive is not very practical since developing countries lack their own technology and importing from developed country is an expensive affair for which these countries do not have sufficient resources. Technological development, which leads to demand for skilled and educated labour, ofcourse reduces child labour. However technological backwardness has been a major obstacle for developing countries. A break-through in this area requires not only infrastructure, trained and skilled manpower but also massive investment. Since savings plus direct flow of investment from abroad generally fall short of investment requirement, technological development capable of rendering child labour redundant, as happened in the West in the post-industrial revolution period, seems not feasible in a large number of developing countries.

Keeping in view the limitation of developing countries, no single approach may be considered preventive for reducing the employment of children, especially in populous countries of Asia, Latin America and or poor countries of Africa. Nor has it been suggested. A mix of measures, particularly preventive measures is to be given a try. However, education and compulsory schooling are more effective and potential than any other preventive measure or approach. An effort on a global scale, such as establishing International Education Fund, has to be made if international community is serious about preventing child labour. The contributors may be member states and international organization as the World Bank, I.L.O., UNICEF and regional organizations, e.g. ASEAN, SAARC, O.A.U. and KFAED, SFD etc. Prevention of child labour for which national commitment and political will are being advocated requires international commitment and international political will as well.

The basic idea of 'rehabilitative approach i.e. protecting children who work' provides a sort of 'recognition' to child labour. It has more relevance in the case of 'providing protective and rehabilitative services', 'providing protected work opportunities', 'correcting the conditions that make work hazardous' etc. Once effort is made to protection of any kind in terms of hazards, it tantamount to recognize child labour not an illegal or exploitative activity. Ofcourse, working children should be rehabilitated and withdrawn from the labour force. The very concept of child labour may be considered socially and legally, a hazard in itself rather than finding the ways and means of reducing or eliminating various types of hazards associated with different occupations and industries. Child labour is a hazard in itself for working children and it must be tackled accepting this concept.

International Labour Organization has recommended the following programmes of action concerning the prohibition and immediate elimination of the worst forms of child labour (ILO, 1999, pp. 11-13):

(*a*) "Identifying and denouncing the worst forms of child labour;

(*b*) Preventing children from engaging in or removing them from the worst forms of child labour, protecting them from reprisals and providing for their rehabilitation and social reintegration through measures which address their educational, physical, emotional and psychological needs;

(*c*) Giving special attention to:

  (*i*) younger children;

  (*ii*) the problem of hidden work situations, in which girls are at special risk;

  (*iii*) other groups of children with special vulnerabilities or needs;

(*d*) Identifying and reaching out to communities where children are at special risk;

(*e*) Informing, sensitizing and mobilizing public opinion and concerned groups, including children and their families." (ILO, 1999).

The programme of action outlined above may be divided into :

(*i*) identification of the worst forms of child labour, (*ii*) abolition of the worst forms of child labour, (*iii*) prevention of children from engaging in the worst forms of child labour, (*iv*) rehabilitation of child workers removed or rescued from the worst forms of child labour, and (*v*) social reintegration.

The first task of the national government for identification is to make a comprehensive survey or listing of those occupations, industries and activities which fall under the category of the worst forms of child labour as per definition of the ILO. This task is neither simple nor impossible. Government machinery can very well cope with the work of identifying the worst forms of child labour and their categories. In India, for example, National Sample Survey Organization of the Government may handle the identification project. Similarly, other countries could use their organizations. However, special emphasis should be given to the informal sector and hence precaution be taken accordingly. Identification also requires special attention for the illegal activities where children are in the most vulnerable situation, such as boot legging, drug peddling, smuggling and child prostitution.

Second step may be to estimate or ascertain the number of children working or engaged in the worst forms of child labour. The governments usually and deliberately try to under estimate the problem due to political and certain international considerations. If the task of estimation is assigned to some NGOs with impeccable reputation and track-record, transparency could be assured. To be fair and transparent, the ILO should, in consultation with the concerned national government, not only assign the estimation work to the NGO but bear the expenses from its buget to ease the burden of a developing country. Its experts in consultation with the national government should chalk out a plan for prevention and rehabilitation of child workers in the worst forms of child labour. However, the implementation of plan would be the sole responsibility of the country concerned.

Social reintegration of children engaged in the worst forms of child labour would be another important and gigantic task where NGOs particularly the national NGOs may play an important role. Here education, formal, informal and vocational comes into the picture. However, no special provisions may be required as the existing infrastructure of the country concerned can take care of the lot for the number would not be very large vis-à-vis the population.

Besides agriculture and domestic sector, most of the children work in the informal sector where the enforcement of child labour laws touches the domain of impossibility. What is, then, the way out? The law enforcement could be possible if informal sector is regulated by means of legalization. The aim of the government should be legalization and regulation of informal sector and not earning revenue since social advantages here outweigh economic advantages. If such an approach is adopted, law enforcement may become a 'thresh hold' possibility.

There are various stages involved in legalization of an establishment or enterprise, such as registration with: (*i*) the municipal council, (*ii*) the commercial register, (*iii*) public promotional institutions, (*iv*) authorization of a unit's location, (*v*) registration with the national and local tax authorities, ane (*vi*) registration with the institutions competent for employment and social security matters (Maldonado, 1995) .

It should not be the endeavour to make registration and licensing so difficult to obtain that the entrepreneurs prefer to keep away from these 'formalities'. The complicated procedure and multiple steps promote corruption and inefficiency as well. In most developing countries, complex and time consuming steps for registration have proved a deterrent. On the contrary, wherever registration is free the rate of compliance has been high (Maldonado, 1995, p.721). It is suggested that minimum number of registrations shall be there and such facilities may be provided by the local municipal bodies. It should be obligatory to get registered for every sort of economic activity, whether located in the house or in an industrial estate. Local municipal's registration unit should report to the district level from where regional office gets the report and these should be sent by the regional office to the national office. Hence, a national register may be maintained.

It may be made mandatory for every unit of economic activity to give a pledge for not employing any child labour, otherwise these could be penalized as per the national child labour laws existing in every country. It may act as a deterrent for many micro enterprises which are always interested in avoiding legal hassels.

Once there exists a national register of all units operating in the informal sector, monitoring and regulation would be possible. The municipal bodies or other similar offices may take care of such units vis-à-vis child labour.

Just to fill up loopholes, education from the age of 6 to say 14 shall be made a national duty compelling parents to send their children to schools so as to avoid penalty or punishment. For the infrastructure, international funding may be made available by the organizations such as suggested elsewhere, i.e., International Education Fund either under the aegis of the existing ones, such as, UNICEF or through a newly created body as an U.N. organ. International commitment is as necessary as the political will in the countries concerned. Compulsory education could not be beyond the reach of poor countries or states, if political will is there. Kerala model has proved it while attaining 100% literacy and primary education whereas the state is neither industrially advanced nor rich in India. "Kerala's achievement shows that universal education can be achieved where there is sufficient political will, even in very poor places" (U.N., 1975). These measures effectively and certainly would check the employment of children and eliminate the worst forms of child labour.

'Choice approach' may be suggested here as the best option. Since no developing country can tackle the problem of child labour, or the worst forms of child labour at one go, that too, *in toto*, it is highly desirable in such circumstances to accord priorities. In case of the worst forms of child labour, if the magnitude is large, occupations or industries may be ordered by the degree of worstness. The most worst forms of child labour should be taken up on priority basis. It may also help in learning lessons for the next stage. However, programme should be time bound and preventive measure be strict, otherwise the problem may have ever increasing bulge. An illustration may help in better comprehension. The industries or occupation in India which have acquired notoriety for employing children in the worst forms of child labour are, e.g., glass industry in Firozabad and *beedi* (local cigarette) making in U.P., Bihar and Andhra Pradesh etc. The former has a high degree of the worst forms of child labour comparing with the latter. It is because work in the glass industry severely affects health and has more hazards like extreme temperature and heat, toxic times etc. Hence, children working in the glass industry should be given priority in the matter of preventing employment and their rehabilitation. Such a 'piece-meal' approach based on choices made shall be more effective and feasible, keeping in view the resource constraints and degree of the worst form of child labour.

'Choice approach' also paves the way for component planning for prevention of employment and rehabilitation programme for child workers engaged in the worst forms of child labour. Every problem has its own 'merits' and hence requires a 'special' treatment. The problem of 'bonded' child labour in, for example, carpet weaving in Bhadoi (India), or Nepal or match-making in Sivakasi is different from that of hired child labour in handicrafts such as brassware industry in Moradabad, India or Jasmine flower collection in regions of Egypt. The point to be driven home is that 'piece-meal' approach to tackle the problem of the worst form of child labour warrants component plan, designed only for one particular occupation or industry rather than a plan in general. Hence, 'ranking' exercise, similar to compute rank correlation, is required based on the degree of the worst form of child labour.

It seems *a priori* a long-term plan but when translated into action, it may take less time than what is visualized. There can not be a very large number of hazardous occupations or industries where children may be engaged. This is in fact the number of hazardous units which should be paid attention.

Moreover, invisibility factor makes the situation worst since large number of units are operating from the houses or at the periphery. Local administration and municipal bodies, local voluntary organizations may solve this problem to a large extent. Educational institutions like senior secondary schools and colleges may also be helpful, if motivated for action in this regard, i.e. spotting the units employing children. Such a scheme involving educational institutions for this cause may be effective and a success in countries having a large network like India. This aspect has to be explored and tried by the governments through administrative machinery existing in every nook and corner of the country.

The basic hypothesis underlying the idea of 'choice-approach', 'peace-meal approach' and 'component planning' may be outlined at this juncture, since the proper foundation has been laid.

LIMITED NUMBER OF HAZARDOUS OCCUPATION HYPOTHESIS

In a developing country, total number of hazardous occupations or industry may not be as large as other and non-hazardous occupations. Hence, child workers in hazardous occupations/ industry are less than their counterparts. It makes things manageable from the viewpoint of identification of hazardous occupations/industries and enumeration or estimation of child workers in hazardous occupations. Being a limited number of such work, ranking as per the 'choice-approach' would not be difficult for prevention and rehabilitation of child workers.

CENSUS HYPOTHESIS

In most of developing countries, census of population is carried out at set interval of time. It has relevance for the enumeration of working children in hazardous occupations. Census exercise is ample proof of existing infrastructure and manpower for the enumeration of child workers. Moreover, census of working children may be made a part of population sensus schedule so data are not only collected but updated as well.

LOCAL BODIES HYPOTHESIS

Since local bodies like municipality, town area committee and municipal corporations etc. exist in every town and city, as is the case in India, and these may be assigned the regulation of informal units in their area. Similar to construction permits/ permission, registration of establishments may be brought in their jurisdiction. Hence, a national register can be maintained. Such a system shall be playing an effective role in the prevention of child labour in hazardous occupations and keep a tag on such units in its area of jurisdiction.

MOTIVATION HYPOTHESIS

Educational institutions like senior secondary schools and colleges may play an important role in identification of particularly 'invisible' units employing children in hazardous jobs, provided that the school and college authorities are motivated enough for the task. A large force of students then can be motivated for the social cause. In India, for example, small savings have been motivated by senior secondary teachers and students. The movement has experienced quite a success. In the same manner, educational institutions may be involved for identification and prevention of child labour, especially in hazardous occupations and industries. These student may become key informants in this regard. A little effort may motivate a large number of volunteers. The educational institutions, if motivated properly can do the job under, e.g., National Social Service Scheme or similar programmes.

All the hypotheses outlined above are from the view point of choice-approach where hazardous occupations and industries are to be identified, prioritized, for the estimation or enumeration of child labour and finally for its prevention. Such a vast force of students along with NGOs may also help in the rehabilitation of child workers through voluntary teaching and monitoring. However, primary requirement is the commitment of the government, its administrative set-up and concerted effort to educate the public and motivate the 'volunteers' for this important social cause. If any government seriously interested in the elimination of child labour, particularly from hazardous occupations and industries, it has to make the task a social movement by involving its own machinery, local bodies, educational institutions and NGOs. Ofcourse, a difficult task but not impossible. And it is in the interest of the nation since child labour shall breed poverty and not affluence.

References

ILO (1999), *Child Labour, Report IV, 2 B*, Geneva, ILO, p. 13.

ILO (1999), *Child Labour, Report IV, 2 B*, Geneva, ILO.

Nangia, P. (1991), "The situation of working children in India," in W.E. Myers (ed.), *Protecting Working Children*, London, Zed Books, 1999, p.51.

Rialp, V. (1993), *Children and hazardous work in the Philippines*, Geneva, ILO.

Rosario, A. (1988), "Ragpicking and ragpickers' education and development scheme in Bangalore city", *Country Reports & Case Studies presented at the Second Regional Conference on Child Abuse and Neglect*, Feb. 8-13, Bangkok, (Thailand).

Conditions of Work Digest, vol X, 1/1991, Part II, Annex III.

Bequele, A. & W.E. Myers, *First thing first in Child Labour*, ILO, Geneva, 1995, pp. 110-17.

Bequele, A. & W.E. Myers, *op.cit.*, pp 29-41.

ILO (1999), *Child Labour, Report IV, 2 B*, Geneva, ILO, pp. 11-13.

Ibid.

Maldonado, Carlos (1995), "The Informal Sector: Legalization or Laissez-faire," *International Labour Review*, Vol. 134: 6, p. 173.

Ibid, p. 721. Burundi shows a very high rate of compliance and it is attributed to registration without any charges.

U.N. (1975), *Poverty, Unemployment and development policy: A case study of selected issues with reference to Kerala*, New York, U.N. esp. pp. 121-126.

8. CONVENTIONS, LAWS AND THE RIGHTS OF THE CHILD

The ILO since its inception in 1919 has been concerned with the problem of child labour by setting a minimum age[1] for working children. However, till the mid sixties it followed a sort of 'sectoral approach' to combat child labour as its corner stone was minimum age for admission to employment in certain sectors like, sea[2], agriculture[3], fishing[4], non industrial sector[5], fishing[6], underground work[7] while revising a few such as sea[8], industry[9], non-industrial sector.[10] However, a landmark in the annals of concerted efforts made by the ILO has been its convention[11] concerning Minimum Age for Admission to Employment, 1973, the ILO Convention 138, adopted on 26th June, 1973. Its recommendations known as Recommendations Concerning Minimum Age for Admission to Employment, ILO Recommendation No. 146 have been concerned with five aspects namely, (*i*) National Policy, (*ii*) Minimum Age, (*iii*) Hazardous Employment or work, (*iv*) Conditions of Employment, and (*v*) Enforcement.

ILO RECOMMENDATIONS NO. 146

I. National Policy

1. To ensure the success of the national policy enunciated in Article 1 of the Minimum Age Convention, 1973, high priority should be given to planning for and meeting the needs of children and youth in national development policies and

programmes and to the progressive extension of the inter-related measures necessary to provide the best possible conditions of physical and mental growth for children and young persons.

2. In this connection special attention should be given to such areas of planning and policy as the following:

(*a*) firm national commitment to full employment, in accordance with the Employment Policy Convention and Recommendation 1964, and implementing measures designed to promote employment-oriented development in rural and urban areas;

(*b*) the progressive extension of other economic and social measures to alleviate poverty wherever it exists and to ensure family living standards and income which are such as to make it unnecessary to have recourse to the economic activity of children;

(*c*) the development and progressive extension, without any discrimination, of social security and family welfare measures aimed at ensuring child maintenance, including children's allowances;

(*d*) the development and progressive extension of appropriate facilities for education and vocational orientation and training appropriate in form and content to the needs of children and young persons concerned;

(*e*) the development and progressive extension of adequate facilities for the protection and welfare of children and young persons, including employed young persons, and for the promotion of their development.

3. Particular account should as necessary be taken of the needs of children and young persons who do not have families or do not live with their own families and of migrant children and young persons who live and travel with their families. Measures taken to that end should include the provision of fellowships and vocational training.

4. Full-time attendance at school or participation in approved vocational orientation or training programmes should be required and effectively ensured up to an age at least equal to that specified for admission to employment in accordance with

Article 2 of the Minimum Age Convention, 1973.

5. (*i*) Consideration should be given to measures such as preparatory training, not involving hazards, for types of employment or work in respect of which the minimum age prescribed in accordance with Article 3 of the Minimum Age Convention, 1973, is higher than the age of completion of compulsory full-time schooling.

(*ii*) Analogous measures should be envisaged where the professional exigencies of a particular occupation include a minimum age for admission which is higher than the age of completion of compulsory full-time schooling.

II-Minimum Age

6. The minimum age should be fixed at the same level for all sectors of economic activity.

7. (*i*) Members should take as their objective the progressive raising to 16 years of the minimum age for admission to employment or work specified in pursuance of Article 2 of the Minimum Age Convention, 1973.

(*ii*) Where the minimum age for employment or work covered by Article 2 of the Minimum Age Convention, 1973 is still below 15 years, urgent steps should be taken to raise it to that level.

8. Where it is not immediately feasible to fix a minimum age for all employment in agriculture and in related activities in rural areas, a minimum age should be fixed at least for employment on plantations and, in the other agricultural undertaking referred to in Article 5, paragraph 3, of the Minimum Age Convention, 1973.

III- Hazardous Employment or Work

9. Where the minimum age for admission to types of employment or work which are likely to jeopardize the health, safety or morals of young persons is still below 18 years, immediate steps should be taken to raise it to that level.

10 (*i*) In determination the types of employment or work to which Article 3 of the Minimum Age Convention, 1973 applied,

full account should be taken of relevant international labour standards, such as those concerning dangerous substances, agents or processes (including ionizing radiations), the lifting of heavy weights and underground work.

(*ii*) The list of the types of employment or work in question should be re-examined periodically and revised as necessary, particularly in the light of advancing scientific and technological knowledge.

11. Where, by reference to Article 5 of the Minimum Age Convention, 1973, a minimum age is not immediately fixed for certain branches of economic activity or types of undertakings, appropriate minimum age provisions should be made applicable therein to types of employment or work presenting hazards for young persons.

IV- Conditions of Employment

12. (*i*) Measures should be taken to ensure that the conditions in which children and young persons under the age of 18 years are employed or work reach and are maintained at a satisfactory standard. These conditions should be supervised closely.

(*ii*) Measures should likewise be taken to safeguard and supervise the conditions in which children and young persons undergo vocational orientation and training within undertakings, training institutions and schools for vocational or technical education and to formulate standards for their protection and development.

13. (*i*) In connection with the application of the preceding paragraph, as well as in giving effect to article 7, paragraph 3, of the Minimum Age Convention 1973, special attention should be given to :

(*a*) the provision of fair remuneration and its protection, bearing in mind the principle of equal pay for equal work;

(*b*) the strict limitation of hours spent at work in a day and in a week, and the prohibition of overtime, so as to allow enough time for education and training (including the time needed for homework related thereto), for rest during the day and for leisure activities;

(*c*) the granting, without possibility of exception, save in genuine emergency, of a minimum consecutive period of 12 hours night rest, and of customary weekly rest days;

(*d*) the granting of an annual holiday with pay of at least four weeks and, in any case, not shorter than that granted to adults;

(*e*) coverage by social security schemes, including employment injury, medical care and sickness benefit schemes, whatever the conditions of employment or work may be;

(*f*) the maintenance of satisfactory standards of safety and health and appropriate instruction and supervision.

(*ii*) Sub paragraph (*i*) of this Paragraph applies to young seafarers in so far as they are not covered in respect of the matters dealt with there in by International Labour Conventions or Recommendations specifically concerned with maritime employment.

V- Enforcement

14. (*i*) Measures to ensure the effective application of the Minimum Age Convention 1973, and of this Recommendation should include:

(*a*) the strengthening as necessary of labour inspection and related services, for instance by the special training of inspectors to detect abuses in the employment or work of children and young persons and to correct such abuses; and

(*b*) the strengthening of services for the improvement and inspection of training in undertakings;

(*ii*) Emphasis should be placed on the role which can be played by inspectors in supplying information and advice on effective means of complying with relevant provisions as well as in securing their enforcement;

(*iii*) Labour inspection and inspection of training in undertakings should be closely co-ordinated to provide the greatest economic efficiency and, generally, the labour administration services should work in close co-operation with the services responsible for the education, training, welfare and guidance of children and young persons.

15. Special attention should be paid:

(*a*) to the enforcement of provisions concerning employment in hazardous types of employment or work; and

(*b*) in so far as education or training is compulsory, to the prevention of the employment or work of children and young persons during the hours when instruction is available.

16. The following measures should be taken to facilitate the verification of ages:

(*a*) the public authorities should maintain an effective system of birth registration, which should include the issue of birth certificates;

(*b*) employers should be required to keep and to make available to the competent authority registers or other documents indicating the names and ages or dates of birth, duly certified wherever possible, not only of children and young persons employed by them but also of those receiving vocational orientation or training in their undertakings;

(*c*) children and young persons working in the streets, in outside stalls, in public places, in itinerant occupations or in other circumstances which make the checking of employers records impracticable should be issued licenses or other documents indicating their eligibility for such work.

The ILO has provided a flexible framework for emanating national legislations to, if not total elimination than, combat child labour. Its Minimum Age Convention, 1973 has been considered as the cornerstone of current international child labour law. The Minimum Age Convention, 1973 and Recommendation provide basic guidelines for eliminating and curtailing child labour, and also guiding countries in framing legislations in accordance with their socio-economic and cultural milieu. It is recognized that "Child Labour laws are essential to deal with the worst forms of child work where they exist and to provide minimum levels of protection where child labour is unavoidable"[12]. To protect the rights of children, laws are essential.

CHILD LABOUR LAWS

Almost all countries of the world have laws against prohibition, and elimination of child labour laws. It is not the endeavour to compile child labour in existence and enforcement in all the countries. But certain countries having lion's share of the problem of child labour merit attention and hence discussion, albeit brief, on their legislations concerning child labour.

India is one of those countries which has a long history of child labour legislation[13] and also ironically largest child labour force in the world. The Constitution of India prohibits employment of children less than fourteen years in hazardous employment, mines and factories. The worst form of child labour is pledged labour where child is pledged for some advance. Hence, The Children (Pledging of Labour) Act, 1933 made this practice illegal. Ironically, there is still a large number of bonded children in India.

Just after independence, a number of acts were enacted in the legislation of India to ameliorate the plight of working children. These were the Factories Act, 1948; the Minimum Wages Act, 1948.These acts were to prohibit child labour in certain employment and also to protect the interest of working children. The employment of children acts were revised in 1949 and 1951. Similarly factories act was also amended in 1954. Since the under ground work such as mining is considered hazardous for children, the Mines Act was enacted in 1952. Other activities where children are employed such as merchant shipping, motor transport were also covered to prohibit child labour.

Informal sector is infamous in every country including India for the exploitation of child labour by means of apprenticeship. Therefore, the Government of India promulgated the Apprentices Act in 1961. Various NGOs have highlighted the employment and thereby exploitation of very young children in *Beedi* and Cigar industries. They work under very harsh conditions and paid meagre wages. Hence, to eliminate child labour in this sub-sector the Beedi and Cigar Workers (Conditions of Employment) Act was implemented in 1966. In the light of experiences, complaints and problems faced by child workers, the Employment of Children Act was again amended in 1978.

A landmark has been the promulgation of the Child Labour (Prohibition and Regulation) Act of 1986 which is an effort to consolidate the various laws pertaining to child labour and promulgated from time to time. This particular Act is comprehensive in the sense that it not only defines child i.e. 14 years or under but also lists occupations prohibited for the employment of child labour, time limit where children are permitted to work, penalties and punishment etc. Consequently, there were a number of prosecutions and convictions under the Act.

The efficacy of the existing legislation and implementation may be judged from the fact that India still has "the largest number of urban and rural child workers in the world"[14].

The National Policy of Child Labour, 1987 aims at eliminating child labour through: (*i*) legislative action plan, (*ii*) general development programmes, and (*iii*) project based plan of action. In regard to the Legislative Action Plan, the Government aims at strict implementation of all legislations concerning child labour and also prohibiting child labour in more occupations.

The National Policy on Education enforced in 1986 has been made a plank of the general development programmes to benefit working children. Schooling, e.g. has to be provided through a non-formal system of education to the children who attained the age of eleven years.

Similarly, where the number of working children is overwhelming, National Child Labour Projects have been initiated. The provision of setting up special school for working children in such sectors and areas/states has also been made.

The Government of India is also participating in the International Programme on the Elimination of Child Labour, i.e., IPEC. The ILO has also started its Child Labour Action and Support Progamme, CLASP in India. However, ever growing number of working children speaks about the colossal problem and not-so-effective legislations and programmes. The lack of political will can be read between the lines.

The Philippines is also known for its severe problem of child labour where the estimated number of working children ranges between 5 and 5.7 million.[15] Child workers are generally working in gold mining, food processing, fireworks, footwear, plastic bags and fishing besides export sectors such as garments, and furniture etc.

The Child Protection Act, 1992 and the Republic Act No. 7610, have set the minimum age at 15 years with certain exceptions. Similarly, the Republic Act No. 7658 and amendment of the Republic Act No. 7610 prohibit labour of children less than 15 years of age. However, legislation has been implemented through the inspectorate system which, keeping in view the scatterdness of informal sector and number of children working therein, would never be effective.

Among other Asian countries Bangladesh is estimated to have a very large number of working children, i.e., 15 million.[16] Another distinct feature is that all the working children in the coutnry's export sector are found in the garment industry.

There is no dearth of the laws dealing with child labour in Bangladesh. The number of special laws and ordinances for the protection of child labour is around 25. The factories Act of 1965 prohibits children under 14 to work in any factory and the law has set time limit for work. Similarly, the Employment of Children Act, 1938 and amended in 1974 has the same age limit for children working in the factories. While other laws such as Shops and Establishments Act 1965, the Children's Act 1974 and Children's Rules, 1976 also aim at protecting working children in different spheres of the economy. However, poor provisions and ineffective implementation have not yielded desired results, nor there is any such possibility in the near future keeping in view the socio-economic problems of Bangladesh.

Latin America is another region besides Asia where the problem of child labour is predominant and colossal. All the big cities in Latin American countries are swarmed by working children under the age of 18. The figure runs in millions for every Latin American country if one goes by the 'guesstimates'. In Peru, official estimate is about two millions,[17] similarly there are around two million working children in Brazil, that too, in the age group of 10 and 13 years.[18] The situation in other countries in this region is no better. In Brazil, Decree No. 66280 specifies the conditions in which children between 12 and 14 years may work; while Decree No. 5798 of 1940 has been amended by Decree No. 50114 in 1961 which is regarding Merchant Marine Regulations. The Constitution of Brazil of 1988 sets the age limit for working children at 14 years (Article 227). While the Statues on Children and Adolescents, i.e. Law 8069-90 later on promulgated as the Law in 1990 adds the conditions for apprenticeship.

It is estimated that there are around 11 million children under 15 years of age working in Mexico.[19] The Federal Labour Law, Article 23 (a) has fixed the minimum age for work at 14 years. The Constitution has special provisions for working children between 14 and 16 years of age. Article 175 bans child labour in dangerous and unhealthy underground or under water works for minors. While Articles 23, 174 and 423 require not only legal permission for work but also regular medical check-up of working children under eighteen. However, enforcement of these laws and provisions have not been effective and failed to yield desired results.

Latin American region, where child labour is largely found in agriculture, plantations and informal sector, has a long way to go concerning formulation and implementation of child labour laws. The governments have not made concerted efforts to enforce legislation since thriving child labour force proves it beyond doubt.

The U.N. Commission on Human Rights has been reported that the working children in Africa constitute around 17 percent of labour force[20]. It is also estimated that the rate of child labour in Africa is highest. Children in African countries mainly work in agriculture, plantations and petty trades falling under informal sector in these countries. In many countries, children wash and watch cars, trade food and perform domestic services in urban areas. While rural area's children have to fetch water even from long distances, collect firewood, herd animals and assist in agricultural activities. However, there is a difference in the perceptions of work in the urban and rural areas. In the urban area most of their activities are earning-oriented whereas in the rural areas, children's work is taken as part and parcel of tradition and social life. In Cote d' Ivoire, for example, child labour has not been considered a serious problem due to general attitude that it is required to assist in farming in the countryside while necessary to avoide starvation in the urban area. Hence, the international organizations including UNICEF and the ILO could not get much public support for the cause. There are minimum age limits for works in agricultural and informal sectors, besides formal sector. It is twelve years in the case of light agricultural work and between 12 and 14 years of age are not permitted without the consent of their parents and that too, for four and a half hours a day. Similarly, the minimum age for domestic services is also twelve years while for other basic works, it is 14 years. Moreover, for underground and hazardous works minimum ages are 16 and 18 years respectively. Child labour laws are strictly enforced in the formal sector but least enforced in the informal sector. It is not due to lack of administration or lacunae on the part of law enforcing agencies, but largely due to the perceptions about child labour. Another startling feature is that nearly 70 percent of Ivorian children leave school at the age of 12-13 while law has made education compulsory till the age of 16 years.[22]

Child labour legislation in Egypt[22] bans child labour under 12 years of age as per the Article 124 of the Labour Act No. 91 of 1959 and for hazardous works, minimum age is 15 years. Another law dealing with child labour, i.e. Labour Law No. 137 of 1981 restricts the work of children, between 12 and 16 years, for six hours a day and in no case after 7 p.m. children of the said age group are allowed to work. In recent years, the minimum age for children legally allowed to work is being raised from 12 to 14 years. Despite all the provisions there are around 1.4 million working children[23], between the ages of 6 and 14, in Egypt showing the lacunae in the enforcing agencies and also reflecting the socio-economic structure mainly responsible for child labour.

For some African countries, authoritative source of information on child labour is available. One such country is Tanzania where around 13.2 percent of children between the ages of 10 and 14 years work in various sectors[24]. The Employment Ordinance No. 47 promulgated on November 10, 1955, amended in 1960, 1962 and again in 1969 sets the minimum age at 12 years while places conditions for children between 12 and 14 years of age working on daily wage-rate. They are, bylaw, required to have the permission of their parents and should be provided transportation to and fro their homes. Stringent laws exist but enforcement does not. Similarly, Tanzania has also framed legislation for its region, *viz*. Zanzibar where the Decree No. 8 of April 1952, was promulgated and then revised, concerning the employment of children, young persons and adolescents.

Another African country for which authoritative source of information exists is Zimbabwe[25]. There have not been specific laws on child labour in Zimbabwe. However, the Children's Adoption and Protection Act of 1972; the Labour Relations Act of 1985 and the Work Act of 1984 restrict certain activities for the use of child labour. This shows inadequacy of laws and apathy towards the use of child labour in Zimbabwe. At present the ILO has been co-operating with Zimbabwe in framing labour laws which will contain laws on child labour as well.

Almost all the countries in Africa have child labour laws. Kenya, for example, which has promulgated the Employment Act No. 2 of 1976, Merchant Shipping Act No. 35 of 1967, Employment (Children) Rules of June 6, 1977 and, Employment of Juveniles at Sea (Medical examination) Rules of June 6, 1977 show the existence of child labour laws. Similarly, Senegal has, especially Decree No. 62-017 of 22nd Jan, 1962, Order No. 3723/IT of Sept. 1954 providing exceptions to minimum age for admission to employment and Order No. 3724 of 22 June, 1954 regarding the employment of children; Madagascar, Ordinance No. 75-013/DM promulgating Labour Code, May 17, 1975 and

Decree No. 62-152 of March 1962 there in covering conditions of work of children; Niger has Act No. 52-12 of July 1962 establishing Labour Code, Decree No. 67-126 MFP/T of Sept. 1967 respecting the regulations of the Labour Code; Zaire establishing Labour code by the Legislative Ordinance No. 67/310 of Aug. 1967, then Order No. 68/13 of May 1968 regulating work conditions of children and Departmental Orders, e.g. No. 28/75 of Oct. 1975 concerning medical examination for job etc.[26]

The situation of child labour in Africa may be summed-up as follows, which was actually reported for Lesotho.

"The Committee notes from the Government report that the inspectorate division of the Labour Department is reluctant to implement the existing provisions of the law relating to minimum age. According to the report, barring persons under the minimum age from employment would deprive them, and often their families, of a livelihood."[27]

THE RIGHTS OF THE CHILD & CHILD LABOUR

"Should the preamble note the provisions of the United Nations Convention on the Rights of the Child and other relevant United Nations instruments?"[28]

The Governing Body of the ILO, following its double discussion procedure, sent questionnaire to the governments of the member states of the ILO as decided at the 86th session of the International Labour Conference in 1998[29]. The total number of replies was 108 out of which : affirmative 103, negative 2 and, other 3. However, one affirmative response was :"Yes" because of the correlation between the rights of the child and child labour"[30]. Is there really a correlation between the rights of the child and child labour? In order to address to the question first the rights of the child have to be dwelled upon. This is nothing short of referring to U.N. Convention on the Rights of the Child. The Principles[31] underlying the Rights of the Children under the 1959 Declaration were:[32]

1. The child shall enjoy all the rights set forth in this Declaration. Every child, without any exception whatsoever, shall be entitled to these rights, without

distinction or discrimination on account of race, colour, sex, language, religion, political or other opinion, national or social origin, property, birth or other status whether of himself or of his family;

2. The child shall enjoy special protection, and shall be given opportunities and facilities, by law and by other means, to enable him to develop physically, mentally, morally, spiritually and socially in a healthy and normal manner and in conditions of freedom and dignity. In the enactment of laws for this purpose, the best interests of the child shall be the paramount considerations;
3. The child shall be entitled from his birth to a name and a nationality;
4. The child shall enjoy the benefits of social security. He shall be entitled to grow and develop in health; to this end, special care and protection shall be provided both to him and his mother, including adequate pre-natal and post-natal care. The child shall have the right to adequate nutrition, housing, recreation and medical services;
5. The child who is physically, mentally or socially handicapped shall be given the special treatment, education and care required by his particular condition;
6. The child for the full and harmonious development of his personality, needs love and understanding. He shall, wherever possible, grow up in the care and under the responsibility of his parents, and in any case, in an atmosphere of affection and material security; a child of tender years shall not, save in exceptional circumstances, be separated from his mother. Society and public authorities shall have the duty to extend particular care to children without family and to those without adequate means of support. Payment of State and other assistance towards the maintenance of children of large families is desirable;
7. The child is entitled to receive education which shall be free and compulsory, atleast in the elementary stages, he shall be given an education which will promote his general culture, and enable him, on a basis of equal opportunity,

to develop his individual judgment, and his sense of moral and social responsibility, and to become a useful member of society;

8. The child shall in all circumstances be among the first to receive protection and relief;
9. The child shall be protected against all forms of neglect, cruelty and exploitation. He shall not be the subject of traffic in any form.
10. The child shall not be admitted to employment before an appropriate minimum age, he shall in no case be caused or permitted to engage in any occupation or employment which would prejudice his health or education, or interfere with his physical, mental or moral development;
11. The child shall be protected from practices which may foster racial, religious, and any other form of discrimination. He shall be brought up in a spirit of understanding, tolerance, friendship among peoples, peace and universal brotherhood, and in full consciousness that his energy and talents should be devoted to the service of his fellow men.

These ten commandments are rhetorically repeated, pronounced and rarely acted upon.

Conventions are binding upon the governments which are signatory to these. In the year of the child, that is, 1979 a proposal was made to have a Convention on the Rights of the Child and ten years later, on November 20, 1989 the 54 articles of the Convention were adopted. It was precisely after thirty years of the adoption of the Declaration on the Rights of the Child. The goal was that all the member countries will have ratified the Convention by the year 1995. However, 188 countries have ratified it by 1996.

The rights of the child as spelled out in the Convention on the Rights of the Child may be broadly categorized into: (*i*) "the right to have basic needs satisfied, (*ii*) the right to protection against exploitation and discrimination, and (*iii*) the right to exert influence through having the opportunity to express an opinion and have it respected".[33]

The U.N. Convention on the Rights of the Child, 1989 has

three Parts. In the Part I, there are 41 articles whose summary is presented below. While Part II and Part III contain four articles, i.e. from Article 42 to Article 45 and 9 articles, i.e. from Article 46 to Article 54 respectively. The first part deals with the rights of the child covering social, economic, political and cultural aspects while the second part provides a *modus operandi* for the State Parties. Last part deals with the organization's responsibilities, functions and duties.

An international organization namely *Save the Children* has briefly described the contents of the Part I of the Convention on the Rights of the child in the following manner:

1. "Definition of a child, which means every human being below the age of 18 unless, under the law applicable to the child, majority is attained earlier;
2. Protection against discrimination, irrespective of the child's or his or her parents or legal guardian's race, color, sex, language, religion, political or other opinion, national, ethinic or social origin, property, disability, birth or other status;
3. The best interest of the child shall be taken into consideration in all actions undertaken by public or private social welfare institutions, court of law, administrative authorities or legislative bodies;
4. *Implementing rights in the Convention*. State Parties shall undertake measures to the maximum extent of their available resources for the implementation of the rights recognized in the Convention;
5. The responsibilities, rights and duties of parents or wherever applicable members of an extended family, legal guardians or other persons legally responsible for the child, who shall be expected to provide appropriate direction and guidance in the exercise by the child of the rights recognized;
6. *The child's right to life and development:* Every child has the inherent right to life and shall be ensured survival and development to the maximum extent possible;
7. *Name and Nationality:* The right of a child to be registered after birth, the right to a name and nationality and the right

to know and be cared for by his or her parents;

8. *Preservation of child's identity:* The right to preserve his or her identity, nationality, name and family relations;
9. *Separation from parents:* The right of children not to be separated from their parents against their will, except if in accordance with applicable law separation is necessary for the best interest of the child;
10. *Family Reunification:* Reunification of family and child shall be dealt with in a positive, humane and expeditious manner by State Parties;
11. *Illicit transfer and non-return of children*: Measures shall be taken to combat the illicit transfer and non-return of children abroad by bilateral or multilateral agreements;
12. *Hearing the child's views:* The right to express his or her views on matters affecting the child shall be given due weight in accordance with the age and maturity of the child;
13. *Freedom of expression:* Includes freedom to seek, receive and import information and ideas of all kinds regardless of frontiers. Restrictions on this right are laws, national security or public order, health and morals;
14. *Freedom of thought, conscience and religion:* Includes parents rights and duties to provide direction to the child in the exercise of his or her rights;
15. Freedom of association and freedom of peaceful assembly with no other restrictions than those imposed in conformity with the law and necessary in a democratic society;
16. *Protection of privacy:* The right of a child not to be subjected to arbitrary or unlawful interference with his or her privacy, family, home or correspondence;
17. *Access to appropriate Information:* Mass media should be encouraged to disseminate information of social and cultural benefit to the child, to stimulate production of children's books, and to pay particular regard to the linguistic needs of children of minority groups;
18. *Parental Responsibilities:* Parents or legal guardians have the primary responsibility for the upbringing and

development of the child. State parties shall render appropriate assistance to parents and legal guardian in performing their responsibilities;

19. *Protection from abuse and neglect:* The right to be protected from all forms of physical or mental violence, injury or abuse, neglect or negligent treatment, maltreatment or exploitation including sexual abuse, while in the care of parent, legal guardian or any other person who has care of the child;
20. *Protecting Children without Families:* The right to care in the form of foster placement, adoption or placement in suitable institutions with regard to the child's ethnic, religious, cultural and linguistic background;
21. Adoption should be made in accordance with applicable law, on the basis of all pertinent and reliable information and with the consent of concerning parents, relatives or legal guardians. Inter-country adoption should not result in improper financial gains for those involved;
22. *Refugee Children:* The right of a child to receive, whether unaccompanied or accompanied by his or her parents or by any other person, appropriate protection and humanitarian assistance when seeking refugee status or when considered as a refugee, including right to reunification with his or her family;
23. Mentally or physically disabled children should enjoy a full and decent life in conditions which ensure dignity, promote self-reliance, and facilitate the child's active participation in the community;
24. *Health and Health Services:* The right to enjoyment of the highest attainable standard of health as well as treatment of illness and rehabilitation of health. This means among others reducing infant and child mortality and combating malnutrition;
25. Periodic review of placement and treatment of children, who have been placed by the authorities for the purposes of care, protection or treatment of their physical or mental health;
26. *Social Security:* The right of every child to benefit from

social security, including social insurance, shall be realized in accordance with national law;

27. *Standard of Living:* The right to a standard of living adequate for the child's physical, mental, spiritual, moral and social development;
28. The right of education, which means making education compulsory and available free of charge to all, as well as secondary, general and vocational education;
29. The aim of education shall be directed at the development of the child's personality, talents and mental and physical abilities, respect for human rights and cultural identity and preparation for a responsible life in a free society;
30. Children of minorities or indigenous populations should not be denied the right to enjoy their own culture, to profess and practice their own religion, or to use their language;
31. The right to leisure, play and cultural activities appropriate to the age of the child and the right to participate freely in cultural life and the arts;
32. *Child Labour:* The right to be protected from economic exploitation and from work that interferes with the child's education or will be harmful to the child's health or physical, mental, spiritual, moral or social development;
33. *Drug abuse :* The right to be protected from the illicit use of narcotic drugs as well as to be protected against being used in illicit production and trafficking of drugs;
34. *Sexual exploitation:* The right to be protected from all forms of sexual exploitation and sexual abuse as well as to be prevented from engagement in any unlawful sexual activity, use in prostitution, pornographic performances and materials;
35. State parties shall take all appropriate national, bilateral and multilateral measures to prevent the abduction of, the sale of or traffic in children for any purpose or in any form;
36. State parties shall protect the child against all other forms of exploitation prejudicial to any aspect of the child's welfare;
37. *Torture, Degrading Treatment and Deprivation of Liberty:* The

right not to be subjected to torture or other cruel, inhuman or degrading treatment or punishment, including capital punishment or life imprisonment. Every child deprived of liberty shall be treated with humanity and shall have the right to legal assistance.;

38. *Armed Conflicts:* The right of persons who have not attained the age of 15 not to take part in hostilities and not to be drafted into the armed forces. The right to protection and care in armed conflicts;
39. *Care for Child victims:* The right to physical and psychological recovery and social integration of child victims of any form of neglect, exploitation, abuse, torture or other form of cruel treatment, punishment or armed conflict;
40. *Administration of Juvenile Justice:* The right to be treated in a manner consistent with the promotion of the child's sense of dignity and worth to reinforce the child's respect for human rights and the fundamental freedom of others;
41. *Respect for existing Standards:* Nothing in the present Convention shall effect any provisions which are more conducive to the realization of the rights of the child and which may be contained in: (*a*) The law of a State Party or (*b*) International law in force for that State"

Article 32 directly refers to the problem of child labour and the Convention calls for protecting children from exploitation. However, the economic aspects have not been accorded that kind of preference which is merited keeping in view its gigantic nature, i.e. child labour has grown over the time and has a cancerous growth in most of developing countries. It should not be taken as negating the value and impact of all the conventions, be it the ILO Convention regarding the elimination of child labour or the UN Convention Concerning the Rights of the Child. In fact, these conventions and other similar efforts like IPEC have not only provided guidelines to solve or mitigate the problems of child labour but created a necessary atmosphere for the creation or elaboration of legislation to combat child labour. In many countries e.g. Zimbabwe, child labour laws have evolved only due to concerted efforts of the ILO. Do these efforts point towards adequacy? Answer is not in affirmative. Still a lot has to be done not only in the field of legislation but also in the area of administration and implementation of child labour laws. Old and outdated inspectorate system has failed miserably in containing the problem especially in the informal sector in every developing country. It is needed to be linked up with the community, somehow. Similar approach is also desired and warranted in the case of agricultural sector where child labour has taken a refuge since a long time. It has to be tackled and regulated in both the informal and agricultural sector since its elimination at one stroke is simply not feasible. Fallacy is to say that the vastness of agricultural sector or its subsistence nature prohibits the enforcement of child labour laws since revenue setup can take care of it if enforcement is properly chalked and laid-out.

Follow-up: what has been the impact of the ILO Convention of 1973 and the U.N. Convention of 1989? Since these are two important milestones in the recent era for eliminating child labour from developing world and an effort towards repositoring the dignity of child by restoring the rights, impact has to be considered in one way or the other. State parties signatory to the U.N. Convention are under obligation to submit a country report within two years concerning the rights of the child. A country report has two parts : *(i)* introductory part containing general information, e.g. geography, demography, political and legal system etc. and *(ii)* The second part specifically deals with various aspects of the rights of the child. The guidelines are issued to State Party for submitting the report. The major components of the guidelines[34] are :-

(1) *Implementation Measures:* It requires information on measures taken by the State in the field of legislation and child policy in accordance with the Convention, and also concerning mechanism to implement and monitor the Convention.

(2) *Definition:* How the child is defined under national legislation so that the difference with the national legislation and the Convention becomes clear and steps may be taken to bridge the gap, if any. This particular

aspect deals with the fixation of minimum age for various purposes, such as, compulsory education, employment, marriage etc.

(3) *General Principles:* Seeking information on measures such as non-discrimination, best interest of the child, right to life, survival and development, and respect for the views of the child etc.

(4) *Civil Rights and Freedom.* It requires information concerning the implementation of the provisions under the head of Civil Rights and Freedom like name and nationality, preservation of identity, freedom of expression, freedom of thought, conscience and religion, freedom of association and peaceful assembly etc.

(5) *Family Environment and Alternative Care:* This contains information on parental and familial aspects e.g. parental guidance, separation from and reunification with family etc.

(6) *Basic Health and Welfare:* Seeks information about health aspects such as services, situation of HIV/AIDS, child care etc. and also concerning welfare aspects like social security, living standard, disabled children and promotional activities etc.

(7) *Education, Leisure and Cultural Activities:* This section seeks information on formal and non-formal education, vocational training, recreation and cultural activities etc. It is also concerned with the compulsory free primary education and schooling of children which is one of the major plank.

(8) *Special Protection Measures:* Information is also sought about children in specially difficult circumstances, e.g. refugee children and children in armed conflicts, juvenile delinquents, sexual exploitation and child labour etc.

What has been the outcome of the Convention on reporting, implementing and monitoring concerning the socio-economic, cultural and other provisions of the rights of the child? Certainly a lot of changes in the existing scenario of the State Parties can not be expected, that too, in their first reporting since harmonization between the legislative frame work, social set-up of a country with that of the Convention is a time-consuming process and also demands the 'will' which quite often lacks due to political reasons governed by socio-economic factors. The *glimpses*, presented below, are from the reports of some state parties which provide the scope for conjecturing picture in their initial stage of implementing the provisions of the Convention thereby making changes in the direction of restoring the rights of the child. Cautions be taken in drawing any inference as these reports have been submitted by the respective governments and hence, are subject to cross-examination.

Vietnam has been the first Asian country to become a party to the Convention in 1990 and also the first Asian country to submit its report to the Committee on the Rights of the Child. The report submitted by Vietnam contained an overview of the situation concerning the Rights of the Child. It provided information on recent laws and policies such as law on the Protection Care and Education of Children of 1991, Law on the Universalization of Primary Education, the National Constitution of 1992 and, draft National Programme of Action for Children 1991-2000.

Under the Law on the Protection, Care and Education of Children, a child has been defined as a person under 16 years of age.

Law and policies have provision for universal access to primary education but lack of infrastructure etc. are obstacles.

Special Protection Measures for children are recognized and implemented. However, much could not be achieved as, for example, there has been an increase in child labour exploitation.[35]

However, the following observations of the Committee make explicit that how far the country has succeeded in the implementation of various provisions of the Convention.

"The Committee expresses its concern about the negative effects of the economic reforms under way in Vietnam on the situation of children..."[36].

Another country Indonesia submitted its report with certain reservations about the Articles 1,14,16,17,21,22 and 29 of the Convention concerning definition of child, freedom of thought, the right to privacy, access to information and media, the best interests of the child and adoptions, refugee children and the right to education respectively. The report has the following highlights:

(*i*) General Measures of Implementation, Definition and General Principles: The Child Welfare Law of 1979, the National Education System Law of 1979, the Population Development and Family Welfare Enhancement Law of 1992.

The definition of a child, under the Child Welfare Law, is 'a child is a person below 21 years of age, unless he or she is married'.

- Compulsory education shall be increased from six to nine years but its drawbacks are high drop-out rate and gender preference for the schooling of boys.

- The labour law prohibits employment of children under 14 years of age. However, some two million children, between 10 and 14 years, are economically active.

How far the situation has improved in Indonesia may be guessed from one of the several remarks made by the Committee, i.e. "The committee is also concerned at the lack of information provided about the situation of child labour and the situation of children..."[37]. The Committee expressed its concern regarding, *inter-alia,* child labour exploitation, inadequate juvenile justice system etc. However, in its final observations, the Committee recognized various positive aspects especially the process of reviewing legislation.

The Philippines, a party to the Convention, submitted its first country report in September 1993. Incidentally, some NGOs also submitted their report but separately.

The Philippines, under the heads of General Measures of Implementation, Definitions and General Principles has informed that the Convention is being implemented through the constitution and various national laws such as, the Child and Youth Welfare Code, the Family Code, the Barangay Level Total Development and Protection of Children Act, and the Special Protection Act. Under national law, a child is defined as a person under 18 years of age, while the Special Protection Act covers children above 18 years who have special circumstances and difficulties. An Education For All Programmes of Action 1991-2000 has been initiated keeping in view the Convention. Children are protected from economic exploitation by the Labour Code, while in future legislation would be framed defining the minimum age for admission to employment in various sectors of the economy and measure shall be taken to protect children from exploitation not only by the employers but also by parents. The employment of children in hazardous work is prohibited and now efforts would be intensified in this direction. However, certain difficulties regarding economic exploitation of children, including child labour have also been mentioned e.g. data deficiency, inadequate enforcement of laws and policies, limited income alternatives for child labour etc. The report, however, admitted that "While the legislative foundation for upholding child rights is well in place, the sad reality is that there is a great distance between enactment of laws on children's rights and the children's enjoyment of these rights"[38]. NGOs, on the other hand, submitted a separate report which is highly critical of the Government.[39] It is not only in agreement with the Government about the gap between law and practice but also hits at the Philippines Plan of Action for Children since, *inter-alia*, monitoring mechanism is not fully operational in the country. It has also criticized the limited access to the early childhood education in the Philippines. It points out the ineffective policies by citing economic exploitation of children since 1.5 million children aged between 10 and 14 years of age employed in hazardous work in 1991, while some 20,000 children were sexually exploited in 1989 and now their number has been estimated around 60,000 in 1993.

However, the Committee noted satisfactorily the government's commitment to child rights and efforts to harmonize national laws with the Convention. It feels that if the new guidelines issued in 1996 are executed effectively, the country will make a good progress.

Thailand, another Asian country known for the vulnerability of children, especially working children and sexual exploitation, has submitted its report to the Committee on the Rights of the Child in 1996, two years later than the due date. However, the report submitted by Thailand is treated as a case study due to its process and structure.[40] There has been a sub-committee on the rights of the child under the National Youth Bureau in Thailand. It is consisted of the representatives of both the Government and Non-Government Organizations. All the guidelines of the Committee were translated into the national language, i.e. Thai and then a seminar was organized to collect information as per the guidelines of the Committee so that the country report shall be prepared and submitted. The organization of the Seminar, co-operation and active participation of NGOs and government agencies helped in preparing and finalizing a transparent country report. It contained all the necessary information hither to not available, problems and short-comings and hence it is considered a case study. This particular process of preparing the country report has set an example for other countries which may have to submit their reports in future.

The contents and structure of the country report submitted to the Committee on the Rights of the Child basically adheres to the guidelines provided to Thailand. It is divided into (*i*) Introduction to Thailand, (*ii*) General Measures of Implementation, (*iii*) Definition of a Child, (*iv*) General Principles, (*v*) Civil Rights and Freedoms, (*vi*) The family Environment and Related Factors, (*vii*) Basic Health and Welfare Services, (*viii*) Education, Leisure and Cultural Activities, and (*ix*) Special Protection Measures. The report under the head General Implementation, Definitions and General Principles raised 'problems and then suggested solutions thus making its reporting and efforts very transparent. Similar approach has been followed regarding Civil Rights and Freedoms, and Special Protection Measures—the most sensitive topic for the Government and NGO representatives. Sub-section dealing with child labour raised the problems as follows:

"Labour inspection is neither adequate nor comprehensive, especially in small-scale enterprises. These enterprises carryout sub-contracted assignments whose outputs and workers are not easily regulated. Besides, there is no legislation to directly protect child labour in agricultural undertaking.

Solutions:

1. Amending child labour protection law by raising the minimum age and reducing their working hours to 6 hours a day.
2. Extending compulsory education from 6 years to 9 years and educating primary and lower secondary school pupils on labour conditions and labour protection before their entry in to the labour market.
3. Stepping up scholarships and educational loans, local job creation, promoting occupational training and management techniques that attract children to self-employment."[41]

An example of transparency may be given from the section on child prostitution as the report says that the statistics "vary from some 23,000 (Govt. statistics) to 800,000 (non-governmental statistics), indicating the unreliability of the figures given."[42]

Since final observations are not available, outcome and follow-up has a little long gestation period. However, country report itself has been taken as a model for other countries which may be submitting their reports in future.

IPEC: Following the ILO Convention No. 138 and its accompanying Recommendation No. 146, commonly known as the Minimum Age Convention, 1973 efforts in the field of eradication of child labour, have been intensified. Since 1990, ILO has enhanced its technical co-operation to enlarge the scope and intensity of action against child labour particularly in Asian countries where around 60 percent[43] of the total child labour is harboured.

The ILO initiated a new programme in 1992 to combat child labour by the name of the International Programme on the Elimination of Child Labour (IPEC). This programme has been launched in some fifty countries, e.g. India, Bangladesh, Pakistan, Nepal, Sri Lanka, Thailand, Cambodia, China, Indonesia etc. The ILO has signed memorandum of understanding (MOU's) with thirty three countries till October, 1998. The main objectives are:

- preventing child labour;

- eliminating the use of child labour in hazardous work and providing them alternatives;

- as a transitional measure towards the elimination of child labour, improvement in the working conditions. The Principles and Priorities of IPEC may be listed as:

Although IPEC aims at total elimination of child labour, however keeping in view the socio-economic and cultural realities existing in a developing country, its principle is world-wide concern and priority to local solutions to combat child labour. Since the problem of child labour is complex and gigantic, it needs careful planning and elimination in a phased manner. Hence, IPEC has accorded priority to withdraw child labour from hazardous and exploitative forms.

The 'worst, the first' calls for elimination of worst forms of child labour on a priority basis. IPEC has given top priority to three target groups *viz.* forced and bonded child labour, child labour in hazardous work, and very young, i.e. under 12 years of age child labour.

Targeting the specific problem and applying phased programme is another major plank of the strategy adopted by the IPEC. It selects particular sector or sectors in a country with a target of reducing the number of working children. The programme also involves other organizations and NGOs to achieve the target.

The IPEC also aims at building on successful experiences by "replicating, expand and sustain them in order to have a lasting impact".[44] The IPEC has established programmes in the following areas : (*i*) Universal compulsory education, (*ii*) Direct support for children doing worst forms of labour, (*iii*) Awareness campaigns, and (*iv*) Poverty alleviation. All these programmes are capable of combating child labour. Compulsory basic education from 6 to 9 years restricts children to get drifted in to labour market and it is considered as the most effective child labour law. Similarly, if alternative sources of income are provided and children in worst forms of labour get rehabilitated, worst forms of child labour may effectively be eliminated. There is lack of awareness about child labour problem itself and legislations concerning with the problem, awareness raising campaigns are extremely important. It may act as a deterrent for the employers.

Child labour issues have to be integrated in poverty alleviation programme as a part and parcel of social and economic development policies and plans since poverty is the root cause of child labour.

IPEC considers (*i*) children and their families, (*ii*) government agencies, (*iii*) employers' organizations, (*iv*) workers' organizations, and (*v*) NGOs as its partner in the elimination of child labour. Every activity under the IPEC revolves around working children hence they and their families have to be involved to make the programme successful. Collaboration with government agencies is necessary to implement not only the legislation and child labour policies but also to prevent the use of child labour with their help and co-operation. Any programme or project has to be implemented through the government agencies.

Action plan implemented by the employer or employers, organization has been successful. The most illustrious example is that of Bangladesh. In 1995, Bangladesh Garment Manufacturers and Exporters Association signed an agreement with the ILO and UNICEF to remove all the child workers under 14 years of age from more than 2000 manufacturing units and these working children were removed and placed in schools. The project has been successful in achieving its initial target while the long-term target or rather aim is to withdraw more than 10,000 working children from garment manufacturing and exporting units of Bangladesh. Moreover, the awareness-raising campaign has made child labour a most sensitized social issue causing immense response in just two years. Hence, it is rightly considered as one of the most successful project launched under the IPEC, in collaboration with the Employers' organization, government agencies, UNICEF and NGOs.

Workers' Organizations or trade unions have a significant role to play. As early as 1866 the Congress of the First International Association of Workers called for an international campaign to stop child labour and demanded legislation to prevent child labour.[45] It was trade union movement which led to the adoption of the first International Labour Convention on Minimum Age for Admission to Employment. Still trade unions can play an important role in the prevention of child labour by monitoring and raising concern about the effective implementation of legislation. In fact, trade unions are the best and most effective pressure groups at national and international levels. Trade unions and employers in the European footwear industry adopted a charter on child labour and have banned the employment of children under 15 years of age[46]. Similarly, International Textile, Garment, and Leather Workers' Federation (ITGLWF) has set the objective of eradicating child labour and has implemented 12 point strategy. Moreover trade unions sometimes exert pressure and do lobbying for the elimination of child labour in a particular sector of a country. The ITGLWF, for example, and its European Regional Organization are "lobbying the European Union to suspend trade advantages to Pakistan until it takes proper steps to put a ban on child slavery".[47]

How can trade unions help in eliminating child labour? Ten step have been suggested in this regard. These are: "(*i*) Investigation; local and national level situation analysis, (*ii*) Institutional Development; establishing structures, e.g. focal points, units, committees etc., (*iii*) Policy Development; developing and reviewing a policy and plan of action, (*iv*) Monitoring; watch-dog role in bringing abuse to light, (*v*) Awareness raising; workers education and public education activities, (*vi*) Campaigning; pressing for enforcement, education, consumer action, etc., (*vii*) Collective Bargaining, collective agreements/codes of conduct, (*viii*) Direct support to working children; developing apprenticeships, education and training, (*ix*) Mobilization; child labour coalitions with NGOs, and (*x*) Utilizing the supervisory machinery of international instruments; trade union reports to: ILO Committee of Experts, Working Groups of Contemporary Forms of Slavery, and the Committee on the Rights of the Child."[48]

Lastly, NGOs are the partner of the IPEC. One main feature of the IPEC, distinguishing it from other technical assistance programmes in the UN system and the ILO, is NGOs have been taken as constituents. When six participating countries namely Brazil, India, Indonesia, Kenya, Thailand and Turkey signed MOU with the ILO, steering committees in each of these countries were established and steering committee in every country has representatives of ministries concerned, employers and worker's organizations and representatives of each of the NGOs participating in the programme.[49]

However, many other partners, in the course of time, have joined IPEC in its fight against child labour. These are media, judiciary, health institutions, universities and parliamentarians.

Role of IPEC providing support to partners: IPEC has been making efforts to strengthen the capacity of its partners by (*i*) situation analysis; to determine the nature and magnitude of child labour problems in a given country, (*ii*) Motivation and facilitation; by encouraging alliances of the ILO constituents since it encourages government for commitments, (*iii*) Institutional mechanism; whereby national steering committees establish national "ownership" of the programme, (*iv*) Educating the public; to raise awareness of child labour issues at national level and also in the community and work place, (*v*) Involving the database; IPEC's Statistical Information and Monitoring Programme helps governments to develop national data bank, (*vi*) Organizing regional training courses; for collecting statistics on child labour and training labour inspectors, (*vii*) Direct action; supporting direct action with child workers and children at risk, and (*viii*) Main-streaming, to integrate child labour issues into social and economic policies, plans and budgets.[50]

Child Labour has no doubt been mitigated to some extent by the efforts of the U.N., ILO and other non-government organizations. But the problem is so complex and task is so gigantic that concerted efforts are required. Simply by declaring the rights of the child, conventions and scattered programmes this problem may not be solved in the near future. The involvement of community is essential otherwise the problem of child labour may persist and even expand not only in dimension but intensity as well. Some 250 million children of the age group 5-14 years are working in developing countries while 50 to 60 million between the age of 5 and 11 years are in hazardous circumstances.[51]

References

1. ILO (1919), *The Minimum Age (Industry) Convention*, Geneva, ILO.
2. ILO (1920), *The Minimum Age (Sea) Convention*, Geneva, ILO.
3. ILO (1921), *The Minimum Age (Agriculture) Convention*, Geneva, ILO.
4. ILO (1921), *The Minimum Age (Trimmers & Stokers) Convention*, Geneva, ILO.
5. ILO (1932), *The Minimum Age (Non-Industrial Employment) Convention*, Geneva, ILO.
6. ILO (1959), *The Minimum Age (Fishermen) Convention*, Geneva, ILO.
7. ILO (1965), *The Minimum Age (Underground Work) Convention.* Geneva, ILO.
8. ILO (1936), *The Minimum Age (Sea) Convention (Revised)*, Geneva, ILO.
9. ILO (1937), *The Minimum Age (Industry) Convention (Revised)*, Geneva, ILO.
10. ILO (1937), *The Minimum Age (Non-Industrial Employment) Convention (Revised)*, Geneva, ILO.
11. See appendix 1.
12. Bequele, A & W.E. Myers (1995), *First things first in child labour: Eliminating work detrimental to children*, Geneva, UNICEF/ ILO, p. 88.
13. ILO (1991), "Child Labour: Law and Practice", in *Conditions of Work Digest*, Geneva, ILO, Vol. 1, p.3.
14. Dingwaney, M. *et.al* (1988), *Children of Darkness: A Manual on Child Labour in India*, New Delhi, Rural Labour Cell.
15. Fyfe, A. (1994), *Child Labour Policy and the Role of Education in India*, Geneva, ILO (*mimeo*), p. 2 as cited in U.S. Deptt. of Labour, *By the Sweat & Toil of Children*, Bureau of International Labour Affairs, 1994, p. 73.
16. Guerro, E. (1993), "Children Victims and Result of Poverty in Philippines", Associated Press, June 30.
17. ICFTU/APRO (1993), *"Country Reports in a Nutshell"*, in sub-Regional Seminars on Child Labour, Oct., Chart1, as cited in U.S. Deptt. of Labour, *op. cit.*, p. 27.
18. U.S. Deptt. of Labour (1994), *op. cit.*, p. 27.
19. Schibotts, G.& A. Cussianovich (1994), *Working Children :*

Building an Identity, Lima, Manthoc, p. 27.

20. U.S. Deptt. of Labour (1994), *op. cit.*, p. 36.
21. U.S. Deptt. of State (1994), *Country Reports on Human Rights Practices for 1993*, Washington D.C., U.S. Deptt. of State, p. 502.
22. UN Commission on Human Rights (1994), *U.N. Doc. E/CN.4/ 1994/84*, p.20
23. U.S. Deptt. of Labour (1994), *op. cit.*, p. 60.
24. Unicef, MOJ (1989), *Child Labour Legislation in Egypt*, Cairo, UNICEF & Egyptian Ministry of Justice, pp. 126-29.
25. Fergany, N. (1993), *Child Labour in the Arab Countries*, the Arab Council for Childhood and Development, p. 14.
26. ILO (1992), *Child Labour in Tanzania*, Geneva, ILO, p. 8.
27. ILO (1992), *Towards Action Against Child Labour in Zimbabwe*, Geneva, ILO.
28. ILO (1981), *Minimum Age*, Geneva, ILO, pp. 179-209 (*List of Legislation by Country*).
29. ILO (1994), *Report of the Committee of Experts on the Application of Conventions and Recommendations*, Geneva, ILO, Report III, Part 4a, pp. 61-62.
30. ILO (1998), *Child Labour*, Geneva, ILO, Report VI (2), Question, 4, p.28.
31. *Ibid*, p.1.
32. *Ibid*, p.3.
33. Ennew, J. & B. Milne (1989), *The Next Generation: Lives of Third World Children*, London, Zed Books Ltd., pp. 16-80 (for detailed discussion).
34. Clason, E. (*n.d.*), *Save the Children and Children's Rights: In a Historical Perspective*, Geneva, 15CA, pp. 17-19.
35. *Ibid*, p. 27.
36. *Ibid*, pp. 28-36.
37. Muntarbhorn, V. (1997), *A Source Book for Reporting Under the Convention on the Rights of the Child*, Bangkok, UNICEF, pp 14-19.
38. *Ibid*, p. 27.
39. *Ibid*, p.29.
40. *Ibid*, p.38.
41. UN (1993), *Doc. CRC/C/3/Add. 23*, p. 54.
42. NGO Coalition for Monitoring the CRC (1994), *Supplementary Report*, Manila, *NGO Coalition for Monitoring the Convention on the Rights of the Child*, pp. 18.
43. Muntarbhorn, V. (1997), *Case Study: Thailand*, in Muntarbhorn, V., *op. cit.*, p. 56.
44. National Youth Bureau (1996), *Thailands' Report on the*

Implementation of the Convention on the Rights of the Child, Bangkok, Prime Minister's Office & NYB, p. 131.
45. *Ibid*, pp. 134-35.
46. ILO (1998), *Child Labour: The ILO in Asia and the Pacific*, Bangkok, the ILO Regional Office, p. 5.
47. *Ibid*, p. 13.
48. Querenghi, G. (1996), "A New Trade Union Onslaught Against Child Labour, in Trade Unions and Child Labour", *Labour Education*, Vol.1, No. 102, p. 1.
49. Kearney, N. (1996), "There is not a moment to Lose...", *Ibid*, p. 8.
50. *Ibid*, p. 10.
51. ILO (1996), "A Framework for Trade Union Policy and Action to Combat Child Labour", *Labour Education*, Vol. 1, No. 102, p. 12.
52. Maier, H. (1996), "Even the poorest people recognize...", *Labour Education, op. cit.*, pp. 2-3.
53. ILO (1998), *op. cit.*, pp. 16-19.
54. UNICEF (2000), The State of the World's Children 2000, New York/Geneva, UNICEF, p. 24.

9. METHODOLOGICAL ISSUES

Standardisation of methodology may not be possible to investigate a socio-economic phenomenon. Research studies of varying nature and objectives apply different methodology. The milieu and surrounding do help in deciding a particular methodological approach to the problem to be investigated. Analogously, end-users also affect decision about methodology, often neglected by researchers in general. However, experts may not afford to ignore end-users and write research report accordingly. Its weightage differentiate government report from that of NGOs and academics. It highlights that construction of methodology to investigate any socio-economic problem depends upon a host of factors. A decision, therefore, about the methods of analysis is also influenced by methodological approach to the problem.

Child Labour is a multi-faceted problem where methodology for investigation may vary from case to case. However, categorization of child labour problem according to nature and objectives would facilitate delineation of methodological approaches and determination of methodology. A qualitative approach to the problem as required and feasible in the case of hidden or invisible child labour guides to a methodology devoid of a common technique of survey and sampling etc. In such a case methods of analysis would be different from that of quantitative approach to the problem of child labour.

Invisible or hidden child labour generally includes child trafficking, child boot legging and drug peddling, child prostitution. All these areas of child labour fall in the risk zone where any investigation or research in a conventional manner is considered dangerous. These are nefarious activities and have involvement of mafioso which can be dangerous for researchers, particularly field investigators. In such circumstances neither methodology based on survey and or sampling is possible nor advised. Moreover, quantitative, in lieu of qualitative, approach to the problem may not yield desired and effective research. Therefore, qualitative research for the assessment and working conditions etc. emerges as a strong probability.

Risk zones in the field of child labour may be studied through observation and discrete investigation which are not commonly applied in conventional research. In such problems key-informants may be most important source of information, and some what reliable, as the best possible approximation of the situation. NGOs active in the area, ex-agents or workers and local journalists may provide vital information in this regard. Area police station are generally knowledgeable and keep tag on such activities officially or otherwise. A close liaison with the police and narcotics officials would lead to better assessment and investigation. Moreover, reliable contacts may be needed to facilitate research in risk zones of child labour problem. But cautious handling and investigation are extremely important.

Conscription of children in outlawed militant organizations or militia and their discrete recruitment even in national armies needs to be investigated. It also falls in the risk zone of child labour problem. Naturally an inquiry and open investigation or formal research would result in denial from those who matter. These are illegal activities by national and international laws and hence admission of such act shall never materialize. Since a large number of children are either lured or forcibly inducted into parallel military output or warring factions, children under arms have to be studied by means of qualitative research methodology based on discrete investigation. In this case key informants such as former child soldiers, trainers and other ex-militia personnel would provide material for research.

Analogously child trafficking, either intra or inter-region, needs to be explored in the sending area and receiving area both. Formal methodology and techniques would be of little help and may endanger researchers and or investigators. Hence, mapping, observations and information discretly gathered from key informants shall form the core of the study. Not only key informants like check posts, area police and social workers would have to be contacted but contacts must be identified and used to facilitate research. Same should be repeated in the receiving area. A direct contact either with mafia, their workers/agents or trafficked children would be dangerous for investigators and concerned children as well.

Children's sexual abuse other than prostitution like pornography either in print media or electronic has caused a concern in the world. Such studies, if undertaken have to be based on observation and key-informant methodology rather than conventional survey and sampling method. Information in this particular case may be collected from those not directly connected with child pornography such as watch-man, film and documentary journalists etc. NGOs working against pornographic use of children would be more informative in facilitating investigation/research.

Another risk zone is children in captivity or semi-captivity where conventional research and methods are ruled out. A number of cases have been reported in the recent past in many countries like Thailand, Philippine and India etc. Such children have been found in manufacturing, fishing and brick-kilns. These children are not allowed to move out of the premises and visitors have no access to them. Their working hours and payments are also irregular. Study of working children in captivity needs a methodology different from common investigation. Once again key-informants are the most important source for researchers. In case of brick-kilns, for example, truck and tractor drivers who carry goods to and from kilns may reveal the inside story. Farmers and labourers in the neighbourhood of brick-kiln can be another source of information. Cattle grazers who roam around brick-kilns may also be contacted in an informal manner to elicit information about children working there and kept in captivity or semi-captivity.

However, it does not mean that a methodology in general may not be suggested. Investigation of child labour problem, not falling in any special category, may follow the methodology delineated below:

IDENTIFICATION

Identification of problem considered to be the first and foremost task of a researcher because a problem not properly identified for investigation may not result in a systematic study. It also involves identification of basic parameters or factors to construct a research study. Moreover, identification entails specification of analysis methods to draw inferences and arrive at conclusion.

In the case of child labour identification of working children according to its functional definition becomes the starting point. Without identifying child labour study on any aspect of the problem is difficult to take-off. It is not simple since child labour is generally prevalent in the informal sector, that is, unregulated and not legalized sector in comparison of the formal sector in the economy. Informal sector has horizontal and vertical scatteredness without any boundaries. It is dispersed in every nook and corner and hence horizontally scattered. While every line of economic activity has vertical dispersion as well. Servicing, for example, has a long down stream and difficult to be traced to the final point. Automobile repairing or servicing may be a good illustration. It has mechanical repairing, interior work, concerned with upholstery, seats and roof laying; body repairing generally known as denting; paint and polishing; auto-electrical work; shocker repairing and tempering; mechanical lathe work; tyre and tube repairing and so on. Then each downstream work in repairing or servicing has its own component or part selling or facilitating activity and the list goes on. In each activity child labour is commonly involved right from apprentice or learner's stage to mechanics. Therefore, a complex and thoroughly scattered nature of informal sector makes identification of child labour a similarly complex task. However, the point here is how to identify child labour for research study.

Some sources supposed to be vital in the identification of child labour for research should be identified keeping in view the nature and objective of a study. Administrative and civic bodies are important as these help in child labour identification. Among administrative bodies police and labour offices, industry office of the government can be contacted to identify child labour, particularly street vendors, petty traders, and children in servicing sector etc. The police keep an eye on street children engaged in street vending and similar activities as they are considered a potential source of trouble from the law and order point of view and nuisance in market and other public places. Labour offices have been entrusted the task of checking child labour commonly found in servicing activities. These do have a track of child workers in the informal sector and semi-formal entities or establishment units. Industry offices generally concerned with manufacturing activity also have an idea about child labour in down and up streams of manufacturing.

Civic bodies like municipality or town area body and municipal corporation generally maintain birth and death records and are important in the sense that these can provide information about children population in their jurisdiction. However, these bodies do not keep information about child labour as such. These bodies also collect information regarding working children in house hold sector which is generally largest sector in any developing country. Therefore, civic bodies can provide valuable information in the case of a study on domestic child labour which is considered as invisible labour. In other cases it may not be an important source of information but should not be neglected in principle.

Voluntary organizations commonly known as Non-Government Organisations (NGOs) and social workers either associated with NGO or independently working are also an important source capable of identifying child labour in various occupations, trades and activities. There are organizations and social workers concerned with child labour *per se* and work for their welfare and rehabilitation. Some of these deal with female child workers and hence have access to them. Such organizations and workers are especially important in the identification of working girls e.g. maids etc.

Other government departments like welfare, and juvenile may also be explored for information on child workers. Juvenile homes which act as corrective and reformative agency have children under eighteen years. These homes shall be integrated into research study from the point of view of identification of working children. Thus, there is a need to explore the records and working of welfare-justice departments so as to identify working children with the help of those children who have been dealt with. This particular source has not been often used in child labour studies in general and identification problem in particular.

Association of traders and manufacturers are common particularly in commercial and industrial cities. These are formed on occupational lines and commercial activities. Informal sector has a significant presence of traders' associations not only on local but regional level as well. The office- bearers are themselves traders and have the knowledge of children working in their respective trade/commerce activities. Hence, urban child labour and even at the periphery of urban centres may be identified with the help of these associations if they are assured of confidentiality and the cause. It's a matter of persuation to exploit this source for identification of working children, particularly feasible for researchers not associated with government departments and or agencies. Independent voluntary organizations, social workers and researchers from academic institution may well convince these associations regarding the cause of child labour and assuring them about no legal action or reprimand. Child labour identification, then, in various trading, commercial and manufacturing activities, and occupations may be facilitated in an effective manner.

Trade unions have legal and other bindings and do not allow for membership to those who are under-age as per the law of the land. Hence, unionism for child workers has neither legal sanctity nor ever attempted at. By virtue of their laws, by-laws, and charter trade unions aim at protecting the interest of workers in terms of working conditions, wages and employment. While child labour adversely affects the interest of trade unions and their members and hence no trade union has been in favour of child labour employment. These unions keep an eye on the direct or indirect employment of child workers and also have a fair idea about their employment in various activities falling in the informal sector. Though such activities are not in the purview of trade unions, these do track down child labour implicitly employed. Therefore, information about child labour may be provided by trade unions and their chapters especially in urban centres for identification purpose.

Community leaders usually know members of their local community and in the neighbourhood. It is especially true in the case of a caste-ridden society. Even minorities are also segmented on the same lines, though they don't have caste system as such. In these societies leaders are invariably there by virtue of either socio-political status or due to religious factor. These leaders are well informed about the activities of their respective communities. In such circumstances they are knowledgeable about children working in different trades, services and manufacturing etc. They would be a valuable source for identification of child labour. Their close contact and frequent meetings with their own community members can lead to child worker's identification.

Occupational dispersion of working children pose the challenge of identification since occupational categories are numerous and hence identifying child labour turns out a complex task for researchers. Community leaders who have knowledge of occupations to which their community belongs may provide substantial information to identify child labour and its prevalence. Therefore, community leaders should not be ignored for the identification of child labour in urban centres and neighbourhood. Group, caste and minority leaders also fall in the category of community leaders and they have to be given a proper weightage in the identification of child labour.

IDENTIFICATION OF CHILD LABOUR LOCATIONS

Next to identifying child labour *per se*, its locations have to be identified. It may be done either by listing or mapping or a mix of both.

Listing means preparing a list of those units falling under various categories such as trade, commerce, manufacturing, and servicing etc. where child labour has been sizable. A classification of economic activities facilitates listing of units engaging child labour in various units of each economic activity. International Labour Organization has been dealing with International Standard Classification of Occupations, and International Standard Industrial Classification which may be used for listing in a scientific manner. These have been revised from time to time according to socio-economic development and hence are more suitable for systematic listing of units which engage working children than other classifications. ILO's classifications are comprehensive and thus leave very little gray area in this regard.

However, functional definitions should be developed for various economic activities and then listing would be logical, for example, establishment has been defined specifically at international level[1] and same may be used for the purpose of listing. Similarly, enterprise and other major heads of economic activity are well defined. Such terms have rather been standardized by one or the other international organization or agency such as UN, UNDP and the ILO, therefore deviation from operational definitions[2] should be avoided until and unless these do not fit into a specific research design. Otherwise results based on arbitrary listing would be questioned from the view point of their acceptability.

Following is the International Standard Classification of Occupations-88 where industrial activities have been classified into categories given below:

(*i*) Agriculture, Hunting and Forestry
(*ii*) Fishing
(*iii*) Manufacturing
(*iv*) Mining and Quarrying
(*v*) Electricity, Gas and Water Supply
(*vi*) Construction
(*vii*) General Trade

(*viii*) Transport, Storage and Communication
(*ix*) Finance and Real Estate Renting
(*x*) General Service
(*xi*) Professional Service

Listing of units engaging child labour may follow the classification of industrial activities given by the United Nations.

Analogously, occupational categories have been enunciated which may be used for listing of child labour under various heads. These occupational categories are:

(1) Legislators, Senior Officials and Managers
(2) Professionals
(3) Technicians and Associate Professionals
(4) Clerks
(5) Service, Shops and Market Sales Workers
(6) Skilled Agricultural and Fishery Workers
(7) Craft and Related Trades Workers
(8) Plant, Machine Operators and Assemblers
(9) Elementary Occupations.

Out of nine major categories of occupations, child labour is ruled out in the first four categories namely, Legislators; Senior Officials and Managers; Professionals; Technicians and Associate Professionals; and Clerks as these have age factor due to either legal provisions or education and training requirement.

These are categories (5) to (9) which have the strong probability of child labour. Among skilled agricultural and fishery workers child labour is being used particularly in fishery work. The famous *Muro- ami* practice in the Philippines is known for child labour where children are used for diving on fishing trawlers. It is not restricted to the Philippines only but several other developing countries e.g. Thailand, India, Indonesia and Bangladesh etc. have child labour in fishery and fishing industry. Children are also engaged in food processing related with fishery.

Craft and related trades have child labour in sizable proportion. Traditional handicrafts are passed on from one generation to the next. India, Pakistan and other developing countries have a number of such crafts where children do work as employment labourers, contract workers and generally as part of the family labour. Carpet industry has employment of child labour not only in India and Pakistan but in Morocco and Egypt as well. Similarly, Zari-Zardozi has child labour in abundance. India's gem polishing industry is another example where child labour is no secret. A long list of craft and related trades can be prepared easily where child labour has been significant. All such crafts and related trades should be listed to identify locations of child labour.

There is a legal restriction to employ or engage children in plant and machine operation but loop holes are there for assembly work. Child labour may, therefore, be found in the assembling units of plants and machines. It would be fruitful to list assembling units for identification of child labour location.

The most important occupations where child labour has been growingly engaged are elementary occupations in most of developing countries. Asia, Africa and Latin America are the regions where large number of child workers are engaged in elementary occupation. Child vendors on street are common in Asia and more visible in Africa while abundant in Latin American countries like Peru and Brazil etc. Similarly, minor mining and quarrying has child labour in a large proportion in African countries. Selling at market places in Africa and Latin America has large number of children. Various agricultural and allied activities like cattle grazing etc. are taken as the work of children in traditional African and Asian societies where it is considered as a way of upbringing of children. Therefore a number of occupational categories and various activities in each category may be listed to locate child labour. Listing would prove an important and fruitful tool of research in the identification of child labour locations in a country, region, city whatever be the case. Listing of all those units where child labour is supposed to exist may be a very useful methodological tool to facilitate research or study, though it has not been often applied. It is one of the most effective way of identification of child labour location and, hence, should be promoted by researchers. A methodology based on listing is equally applicable in enumeration and sampling of child labour. And it leaves no room for chance factor, that is, listing would not have the problem of missing some localities, occupations and industrial activities.

MAPPING

Mapping is another method of identification and leads to systematic research. It depends upon the approach to the problem. Suppose mapping of those location is to be done where child workers are commonly found then mapping would prove effective in the identification of these locations. Firstly, locations as per classification may be mapped. Industrial units falling under various and pre- determined categories of informal units may be located by means of mapping. For example, trading and commercial activities, manufacturing, crafts, and servicing etc. are important activities from the view point of child labour and their mapping would facilitate the analysis. This type of mapping falls in the category of locational mapping for identification of child labour.

Similarly, occupational mapping may also be tried to identify niche of child labour. It would also help in locating child labour engaged in various occupations. Here a mix of locational and occupational categories should be applied to get effective results.

Mapping may also be according to the proportion of child labour in total labour. In such cases a map may demarcate not only area, occupation and activities but also proportions of child labour. It is a technique generally used in physical maps in India and other countries. Any cartographic method may be applied for mapping purpose.

Listing and mapping both are applicable for studies at local, regional and country levels. These methods should be tried at for a systematic study on child labour which may be updated in future as well. It would be a sort of permanent record for future and further research and studies on child labour.

Since child labour is largely in the informal sector scattered all over, it has a very high degree of dispersion in every country. However, whatever methods and procedures are applied to identify locations of child labour, some locations always have a strong probability. Such locations where child labour is supposed to exist are described below for which mapping may be done, though proportion of child in total labour may vary depending upon socio-economic milieu. However, these location may be categorized into two: fixed locations, and floating locations.

'FIXED' LOCATIONS OF CHILD LABOUR

Following are the common fixed locations where child labour exists in sizable proportion.

Commercial Centres

Child labour is predominantly found at commercial centres such as markets either regulated or unregulated. At market places children are engaged and fall in the categories of wage employment, self-employment and, family labour. Those who are hired either on daily wage or monthly salary belong to wage-employment category including those who work as helpers during market hours, that is, morning till late evening every day. They assist at the shop and may be assigned any work.

Children at commercial centres may be seen sellingt it-bits, food articles and other consumption goods and are not hired may be placed in the category of self-employment. Similarly, children selling goods vegetable and grains etc. either produced by their family or purchased from the market may be found in unregulated markets. They are also self-employed but do not have any fixed working hours. In such a case need and convenience both affect their working hours.

Children as part of family labour are found at commercial centres assisting their parents. They help in running shops and also used in stop-gap arrangements. Child family labour has irregular working hours and may not be a regular feature at market places. However, its existence, though insignificant, but may not be denied.

In all the cases, however, children work at the cost of either education or recreation and leisure. Therefore, it falls in the definition of child labour.

Other activities and more exploitative in nature of child labour are weight/load carrying, car washing or dusting, servicing in one or the other form are associated with commercial centres. It is never a rare site at commercial centres to see children as errand boys. Their working hours are long and working conditions are least favourable to them. They also bear the vargaries of weather and have no facility worth its name. These activities are, however, a mix of hired and self-employment.

Repairing centres in urban area thrive upon child labour as it comes by cheap and easy. All the cities and towns have repairing shops, commonly known as workshops where children are employed under the guise of 'learners' or 'apprentices'. All the backstreet sweat shops fall under this category. Children are generally unpaid or nominally paid workers at such work places. Skill acquisition is the main objective for which parents send their children to workshops. They usually fall in the age group of 9-15 years.

In all such cases listing method is more effective to study socio-economic conditions of child workers.

FLOATING LOCATIONS OF CHILD LABOUR

Children in some cases work not at any fixed place but keep on shifting and the most illustrious example is that of ragpickers. They move on from one garbage site to another to collect recycleable wastes, such as polythene, plastic, rubber, glass and metals etc. Dumping sites in India and the Philippine etc. are work place where a number of children from 5 to 15 years may be seen collecting 'useful' garbage.

Similarly, junk dealers collect material like bottles, plastic and polymer canes, iron and other metals etc. from different localities in the city. Some purchase old newspapers and other used paper materials such as books, magazines etc. Children have been engaged in these activities. Such child workers are not found at fixed locations as they keep on moving from place to place.

Nomads particularly Rajasthani nomad move from one city to another as they do not settle at one place. Their children work to manufacture home made utilities for domestic and agricultural purpose, e.g., Knives, hand-shoe, showels etc. or sometimes do manual labour provided that their tribe stays there for a month or so.

In the case of child workers at floating locations study becomes a difficult task for researchers and investigators. Analogously those nomads which move alongwith their cattle-herds in search of pastures and water-holes are not easily traced and difficult to study. *Vana-gujjars* in India is one of those tribes.

IDENTIFICATION OF KEY-LOCATIONS

Some Key- locations may, however, be identified where child labour is supposed to be in a large proportion. It is a broad categorization and may differ according to socio-economic milieu. Moreover, the list is not exhaustive but suggestive in nature. The key locations may be:

(*a*) Back street enterprises,
(*b*) Market places,
(*c*) Cottage industries
(*d*) Transport centres
(*e*) Industrial area
(*f*) Commercial sex area
(*g*) Handicraft centres
(*h*) Farms & plantations
(*i*) Waste disposal sites
(*j*) Service sector

Informal sector, that too, marginal activities largely employ child labour. Such units engaged in marginal manufacturing activities commonly termed as 'back street' enterprises thrive upon child labour due to easy availability and cheap source of labour. These include repairing, workshops and other marginal manufacturing.

Market places and plazas usually have child workers for general assistance, load carrying, wait and watch services and vending. Latin American and African countries have a large number of children engaged in such activities.

Cottage industry in India and elsewhere have a significant presence of child labour. One important reason has been the occupation itself where skill is passed on from one generation to the next. Secondly, this sector heavily depends upon the family labour. Moreover, contractual system has also promoted child labour. Traditional crafts such as *Zari-Zardozi, Kar-chobi* etc. thrive upon work assigned to households of artisans where children largely do the work.

Transport centres especially large distance and goods carrier have a large scope for child labour. In the vicinity minor servicing centre develop where children are employed as errand boys, apprentices and for general assistance. Vending activity also gets promoted in such places due to marginal nature of economic activities.

Industrial Estates generally have ancillary units and satellite service centres where child labour is hired by informal units for general assistance and errand activities. They come from the city and also from the nearby rural area. In fact in such places child workers from rural background are more common since industrial estates have been established at the outskirt of cities.

Child sex workers are growing in number due to wrong placed perception of clients that younger the sex partner, the better. Inter- and intra-region trafficking has been the most important source of supply of child sex workers in commercial sex areas. It is easy for agents to lure children to get them employment in cities and they fall prey to it.

A maximum number of child workers is found in the rural sector of India and other developing countries. Children as family labour and hired workers are engaged in agricultural activities and plantation. No estimates are available in this regard but their 'guesstimates' run into millions.

Dumping sites of municipal and household waste attract children from lower strata of the society to eke out their living. A large number of children engaged in ragpicking may be seen at waste disposal sites generally in the outskirts of cities. The classical exampled of 'Smoky Mountain' in the Philippines is not an isolated one. Such dumps may be seen in most of the cities. Children of various age groups search there for recycleables like plastic, rubber, polythene etc. to sell these articles to junk dealers in the city.

Special mention goes to children engaged in the service sector. It is essentially an urban phenomenon where children from the age of 5 years work in tea stalls, way- side eating places, repairing shops etc. They are in large number and engaged as errand boys. Automobile repairing shops, commonly known as workshops have children to learn the skill and are unpaid employees. They are, in some cases, paid nominal amount as pocket money but have to work for long hours and under poor working conditions. Child labour has long been employed in automobile repairing units and used to run errands or for general assistance. Since 'learning' process is long they stay in such units for a number of years without any worth while remuneration.

IDENTIFICATION OF RESEARCH METHODS

Once methods to identity working children and locations are identified the next logical step is to decide method to study the subject, that is, child labour.

There are no hard and fast rules to apply any particular method of study. However, some commonly applied methods may be listed in the following manner:

Enumeration/Census

Information on child labour may be collected through complete enumeration or census provided that sufficient resources are available and purpose is to cover all the child workers in the area of study.

Since enumeration of or census on child labour is beyond the scope of an individual researcher except in the case of micro study, it is rarely applicable. Only governments and organizations with enough financial and human resources may venture into enumeration. However, importance of enumeration or census can not be negated if total number of child workers is to be ascertained. It is one of the problem which had not been solved and developing countries have, including India, to rely on estimates (Antony *et. al.*, 2003). A number of countries lacking even basic data work on *guesstimates*, not considered reliable in any manner. The solution to the problem thus indicates that enumeration or periodic census is required, if serious effort has to made either to ascertain the number in order to measure the extent of child labour problem or for rehabilitation of child workers.

The census of population has failed to enumerate child labour in the country. It includes children working inside the household and children working in self-employment (Census of India, 1981). A detailed format should be developed and incorporated in the census schedules and thereby in the report for periodic ascertaining of child workers in various sectors of the economy to dispense with estimation which has always been controversial. The magnitude of the problem has not been a settled issue so far (Lieten, 2001).

Micro level studies may however, be pursued individually for enumeration of child workers falling under various age groups and economic activities. Academia as such should strengthen this aspect of child labour as it has the potential as well as the scope and means. But macro studies at individual level are simply not possible for enumeration of child labour at either state or national level. It is a serious handicap of a research methodology on child labour not based on census.

SURVEY

The most effective method of estimating child labour has been survey, though not free from subjectivity. Due to affordability factor survey technique has generally been used by researchers and organizations. However, survey invariably involves sampling since a fraction may be covered at macro level.

Sampling methods are numerous and the use of a particular sampling method depends upon a host of factors. Size of sample is not to be overlooked and any arbitrary number may not serve the purpose of survey as it does not confirm *the law of large numbers*. Researchers for their convenience, sometimes, fix an arbitrary number say hundred or five hundred to cover in their survey. Such absolute numbers, fixed arbitrarily, caste aspersion on the validity of inferences.

Number of child workers is large enough and hence a percentage of it may be sampled rather than any absolute number. The former even very small, determines the size of sample but the latter does not. Here the type of sampling is not questioned but the size is. It is generally overlooked or has little emphasis while involving the validity of results and inferences.

Other aspect requiring careful attention is the method of sampling. A commonly pursued and ofcourse effective method has been questionnaire or interview schedule. But the question is who should be interviewed or to be asked for information and why? General practice is to interview the subject, e.g., child worker. In such case a problem crops up that is how to corroborate information provided by a child worker: Information collected from any source is better to be corroborated from some other source. Moreover, it may be one sided and subject to bias. A child worker may, for example, provide information from his/her point of view while employer's version could be different. It would be, thus, better to gather information so the degree of bias may be minimized, if not over-ruled.

Key- informants would give a balanced view of the problem. In rapid assessment surveys, *key-informants* are the major source of information and more reliable as well. It is one of the important source where information is sought from knowledgeable and reliable persons. They may not be directly linked with persons about whom information is sought. In case of child labour, *key-informants* may be social workers, community leaders, NGOs, personnel of labour department, local intelligence unit, priests and so on. Information revealed by them would not be biased either against child workers or employers.

Key-informant method of survey is being considered as the most- effective in terms of time, energy and cost since neither the size of sample is large nor it takes time as it is in the case of conventional survey. Moreover, inferences drawn on the basis of information provided by *key- informants* would be, more or less, as reliable as given by any large scale survey. Therefore, *key-informant* method of survey on sensitive issues like child labour is being advocated.

Certain areas in the field of child labour are extremely sensitive and need careful probe. Child sex workers is for example one of those area where conventional approach and investigation may not be either possible or fruitful. Investigation of such problems may find *Key-informant* method as the only option. However, methodology and tools can not be standardized and would vary from case to case.

NOTES

1. U.N. (1990), "International Standard Industrial Classification for All Economic Activities", *Statistical Papers,* Series M, No.4, Rev. 3, Doc. ST/ESA/STAT/SER, M/4/Rev.3, New York, U.N. esp. Ch. V.
2. *Ibid,* p. 19.

REFERENCES

Antony, P. and V. Gayathri (2003), "Child Labour: A Perspective of Locale and Context" in *Economic & Political Weekly,* Vol. XXXVII, 52, 2003, p. 5186.

Govt. of India (1981), *Census of India 1981,* Govt. of India, Vol. 22, Part IV-A : 13.

Leeten, G.K. (2001): "Child Labour, Questions on Magnitude", in Leeten and White, *Child Labour, Policy Perspective,* Aksant Academic Publishers, Amsterdan, pp. 47-66.

CONVENTION CONCERNING THE PROHIBITION AND IMMEDIATE ELIMINATION OF THE WORST FORMS OF CHILD LABOUR, 1999.

Article 1

Each member which ratifies this Convention shall take measures to secure the prohibition and immediate elimination of the worst forms of child labour.

Article 2

For the purposes of this Convention, the term "child" shall apply to all persons under the age of 18.

Article 3

For the purposes of this Convention, the expression "the worst forms of child labour" comprises:

(*a*) all forms of slavery or practices similar to slavery, such as the sale and trafficking of children, forced or compulsory labour, debt bondage and serfdom;
(*b*) the use, procuring or offering of a child for prostitution, for the production of pornography or for pornographic performances;
(*c*) the use, procuring or offering of a child for illicit activities, in particular for the production and trafficking of drugs

as defined in the relevant international treaties;

(*d*) work which, by its nature or the circumstances in which it is carried out, is likely to jeopardize the health, safety or morals of children.

Article 4

1. The types of work referred to under Article 3(d) shall be determined by national laws or regulations or by the competent authority, after consultation with the organizations of employers and workers concerned, taking into account relevant interenational standards.
2. The competent authority, after consultation with the organization of employers and workers concerned, shall identify where the types of work so determined exist.
3. The list of types of work determined under paragraph 1 of this Article shall be periodically examined and revised as necessary, after consultation with the organizations of employers and workers concerned.

Article 5

Each Member shall establish or designate appropriate mechanism to monitor the implementation of the provisions giving effect to this Convention.

Article 6

1. Each Member shall design and implement programmes of action to eliminate as a priority the worst forms of child labour.
2. Such programmes of action shall be designed and implemented in consultation with relevant government institutions and employers and workers organizations.

Article 7

1. Each Member shall take all necessary measures to ensure the effective implementation and enforcement of provisions giving effect to this Convention including the

provision and application of penal sections or, as appropriate, other sanctions.

2. Each Member shall, taking into account the importance of education in eliminating child labour, take effective a time-bound measures to:
   (*a*) prevent children from engaging in the worst forms of child labour;
   (*b*) provide the necessary and appropriate direct assistance for their removal from work, rehabilitation and social reintegration through, *inter alia*, access to free basic education;
   (*c*) identify and reach out to children at special risk; and
   (*d*) take account of the special situation of girls.
3. Each Member shall designate the competent authority responsible for the implementation of provisions giving effect to this Convention.

Article 8

Members shall take steps, as appropriate, to assist one another in giving effect to the provisions of this Convention through international cooperation or assistance.

Recommendation concerning the prohibition and immediate elimination of the worst forms of child labour:

1. The provisions of this Recommendations supplement those of the Immediate Abolition of the Worst Forms of Child Labour Convention, 1999 (Here after referred to as : "The Convention"), and should be applied in conjunction with them.

I. Programmes of Action

2. The programmes of action referred to in Article 6 of the Convention should be designed and implemented in consultation with relevant government institutions, employers and workers organizations and, as appropriate, other concerned groups. They should aim at, *inter alia*:

(a) identifying and denouncing the worst forms of child labour;

(b) preventing children from engaging in or removing them from the worst forms of child labour, protecting them from reprisals and providing for their rehabilitation and social reintegration through measures which address their educational, physical, emotional and psychological needs;

(c) giving special attention to

(*i*) young children;

(*ii*) the problem of hidden work situations, in which girls are at special risk;

(*iii*) other groups of children with special vulnerabilities or needs.

(d) identifying and reaching out to communities where children are at special risk;

(e) informing, sensitizing and mobilizing public opinion and concerned groups, including children and their families.

II. Hazardous Work

3. In determining the types of work referred to under Article 3(d) of the Convention, and in identifying where they exist, consideration should be given, as a minimum, to:

(*a*) work which exposes children to physical, emotional or sexual abuse;

(*b*) work underground, under water, at dangerous heights or in confined spaces;

(*c*) work with dangerous machinery, equipment and tools, or which involves the manual handling or transport of heavy loads;

(*d*) work in unhealthy environment which may, for example, expose children to hazardous substances, agents or processes, or to temperatures, noise levels, or vibrations damaging to their health;

(*e*) work under particularly difficult conditions such as

work for long hours or during the night or work which does not allow for the possibility of returning home each day.

III. Implementation

4. (1) Detailed information and statistical data on the nature and extent of child labour should be compiled and kept up to date to serve as a basis for determining priorities for national action and immediate elimination of its worst forms.

   (2) As far as possible, such information and statistical data should include data disaggregated by sex, age group, occupation, branch of economic activity and status in employment.

   (3) Relevant data concerning violations of national provisions for the prohibition and immediate elimination of the worst forms of child labour should be compiled and kept up to date.
5. The compilation and processing of the information and data referred to in Paragraph 4 above should be carried out with due regard for the right to privacy.
6. The information compiled under paragraph 4 should be communicated to the International Labour Office on a regular basis.
7. Members should establish or designate appropriate national mechanism to monitor the implementation of national provisions for the prohibition and immediate elimination of the worst forms of child labour after consultation with employers' and workers' organization and as appropriate, other concerned groups.
8. Members should ensure that the competent authorities which have responsibilities for implementing national provisions for the prohibition and immediate elimination of the worst forms of child labour cooperate with each other and coordinate their activities.
9. National laws or regulations or the competent authority should determine the persons to be held responsible in

the event of non-compliance with national provisions for the prohibition and immediate elimination of the worst forms of child labour.

10. Members should, in so far as it compatible with national law, cooperate with international efforts aimed at the prohibition and immediate elimination of the worst forms of child labour by:
    (*a*) gathering and exchanging information concerning criminal offences, including those involving international networks;
    (*b*) detecting and prosecuting those involved in the sale and trafficking of children, or in the use, procuring or offering of children for illicit activities, for prostitution, for the production of pornography or for pornographic performances; and
    (*c*) registering perpetrators of such offences.
11. Members should provide that the following worst forms of child labour are criminal offences:
    (*a*) all forms of slavery or practices similar to slavery, such as the sale and trafficking of children, forced or compulsory labour, debt bondage and serfdom;
    (*b*) the use, procuring or offering of a child for prostitution, for the production of pornography or for pornographic performances; and
    (*c*) the use, procuring or offering of a child for illicit activities, in particular for the production and trafficking of drugs as defined in the relevant international treaties.
12. Members should ensure that penalties including, where appropriate, criminal penalties are applied for violations of the national provisions for the prohibition and immediate elimination of any type of work referred to in Article 3(d) of the Convention.
13. Members should also provide for other remedies, where appropriate, to ensure the effective enforcement of national provisions for the prohibition and immediate elimination of the worst forms of child labour.
14. Other measures aimed at the prohibition and immediate

elimination of the worst forms of child labour might include the following:

(*a*) informing and sensitizing the general public, including national and local political leaders, parliamentarians and the judiciary;
(*b*) involving and training employers and workers organizations and civic organizations;
(*c*) providing appropriate training for concerned government officials, especially inspectors and law enforcement officials, and for other relevant professionals;
(*d*) providing for the prosecution in their own country of the Members' nationals who commit offences under national provisions for the prohibition and immediate elimination of the worst forms of child labour even when these offences are committed in another country;
(*e*) simplifying legal and administrative procedures and ensuring that they are appropriate and prompt;
(*f*) giving publicity to best practices on child labour;
(*g*) giving publicity to legal or other provisions on child labour in different languages and dialects;
(*h*) establishing special complaints procedures and making provisions to protect those who legitimately expose violations of the provisions of the Convention from discrimination and reprisals, as well as establishing help or points of contact and *ombudspersons*.

15. International cooperation or assistance among Members for the prohibition and immediate elimination of the worst forms of child labour should include:

(*a*) mobilizing resources for national or international programmes;
(*b*) mutual legal assistance;
(*c*) technical assistance including the exchange of information.

Source: ILO, Child Labour, Report IV (2B), Geneva, ILO, pp. 6-17.

In North African countries such as Egypt and Morocco, in handicraft including export carpet export industries, use more child labour overtly or covertly. While the rest of countries have child labour in their garment, textile and mining based export industries. Child labour laws are usually ignored by the enforcement agencies on the plea of poverty and unemployment. Moreover, the perception of child labour is different in Africa than in the West since integration of child labour into adult labour is neither considered detrimental to the growth of child, nor against the norms of the society. On the contrary, child labour has social sanctions being a gradual process of assimilating children into productive work. Lack of educational facilities, and prevalence of unemployment coupled with widespread poverty and harsh conditions, natural, geographical and otherwise, have promoted the use of child labour as a gradual process of integrating it into adult labour. On to this perception, there is not much concern for child labour in many African countries as they have for street children.

There are as many as eight occupations/industries which may cause musculo-skeletal diseases, and even bodily deformation, while the same number of occupations could cause respiratory diseases and also chemical poisoning among the workers, particularly child workers who are more susceptible. Some other risks, having high probability are cuts, burns, injuries stress and strain, and accidents causing severe injuries and often leading to death. These dangers should not be undermined for working children due to their age, capability of judgments for taking precautions against hazards. Moreover, exposure to extreme heat, dust, fumes and radiation cause serious health problems which eventually reduces the life expectancy of children working in such industries or occupation. Such occupations as per the recent convention of the ILO must be taken care of on a priority basis and employment of children, in any form, be immediately banned. There is also a need to educate not only the employers and parents but also children in such occupations about the health and moral hazards. Unless provisions of exemplary punishment for the employers and compensatory or alternative for children working in these occupations are made, worst forms of child labour may go on persisting especially in populous and poor countries causing irreparable damage to the future work force.

A rehabilitative measure could be provision of special school for children released from hazardous occupations or industries. To compensate their parents who are deprived of their children's income, scholarships in case may be given, which in turn, could act as incentive to avail the facility of free and special schooling. Special budgetary allocation just for few years may solve the problem, provided that the employment of children in future is strictly banned through socio-legal measures. But whatever be the provisions, political will is invariably required to the successful implementation and fruitful results.

REFERENCES

AAFLI (1994), *A Report on Child Labour in Pakistan,* Asian-American Free Labour Institute, pp. 5-6.

Abdallah, A. (1988), "Child Labour in Egypt: Leather Tanning in Cairo", in Alec fyfe, *Combating Child Labour,* Geneva, ILO, pp. 33-34.

Aboagye, A.A. & K.M. Gozo (1986), *op. cit.,* p. 264.

Aboagye, A.A. & K.M. Gozo (1986), *op. cit.,* pp. 264-65.

Aboagye, A.A. & K.M. Gozo (1986), "The Informal sector: A Critical Appraisal of the Concept" in *JASPA (ed), The Challenge of Employment & Basic Needs in Africa,* Nairobi, Oxford University Press, p. 265.

Anti-Slavery Society (1978), *Child Labour in Morocco's Carpet Industry,* London (mimeo).

Anti-Slavery Society (1991), *Children in Bondage: Slaves of the Subcontinent, London,* Anti-Slavery Society, p. 24.

Antony, P. and V. Gayathri (2003), "Child Labour: A Perspective of Locale and Context" in *Economic & Political Weekly,* Vol. XXXVII, 52, 2003, p. 5186.

As cited in the U.S. Deptt. of Labour (1994), *op. cit.,* p. 95.

Azer, A. (1990), *Child Labour in Egypt,* Cairo, UNICEF/ NCSCR.

Azer, A. et al. (1993), *Training and Welfare of Working Children in Shubra El Kheima,* Cairo, ILO/NCSCR.

Bangladesh Bureau of Statistics (1992), *Report on Labour Force Survey 1989: Trend of Civilian Labour Force,* Dhaka, B.B.S. xiii, 38-39.

Banpasirichote, B & A Pongsapich (1992), *Child Workers in Hazardous Work in Thailand,* Chulalong korn University Social Research Institute, pp. 42-46.

Based on observations in Bareilly and nearby towns where the author resides. All details of modus operandi were provided by the contractor by the name of Naeem who himself has become an exporter.

Bekombo, M. (1981), "The Child in Africa : Socialization, Education and Work", in Rodgers & G. Standing, *op.cit.*, p. 117.

Bequele, A & W.E. Myers (1995), *First things first in child labour: Eliminating work detrimental to children*, Geneva, UNICEF/ ILO, p. 88.

Bequele, A. & W.E. Myers, *First thing first in child labour*, ILO, Geneva, 1995, pp. 110-17.

Bequele, A. & W.E. Myers, *op.cit.*, pp. 29-41.

Bhowmit, S.K. (1992), "Plantation Labour Act and Child Labour", *Economic & Political Weekly*, vol. xxvii; 42, Oct. 17.

Bonnet, M. (1993), "Child Labour in Africa", *International Labour Review*, Vol. 132 (3), p. 382.

Bonnet, M. (1993), "Child Labour in Africa", *International Labour Review*, vol. 132: 3, pp. 382.

Bromley, R (1978), "Introduction-The urban informal sector : Why is it Worth Discussing"?, *World Development*, pp. 1033-39.

Bromley, R. (1995), "The Urban Informal Sector", in J. Ennew (ed), *Learning or Labouring?*, Florence, UNICEF, p. 10.

Bromley, R. (1995), *op. cit.*, p. 10.

Burra, N. (1986), "Child Labour in India: Poverty, Exploitaton and Vested Interest", *Social Action*, 36, July-Sept., p. 248.

Burra, N. (1988), "Exploitation of Children in Jaipur Gem Industry: Health Hazards of Gem Polishing", *Economic & Political Weekly*, Jan. 23, pp. 135-6.

Burra, N. (1988), "Exploitation of Children in Jaipur Gem Industry II: Health Hazards of Gem Polishing", *Economic & Political Weekly*, Jan. 23, pp. 135-6.

Burra, N. (1989), *Child Labour in the Brassware Industry of Moradabad*, ILO/Asian Regional Team for Employment Promotion, p. 15.

Burra, N. (1991), *Child Labour in the Gem Polishing Industry in Jaipur*, Noida (U.P.), N.L.I., Child Labour Cell.

Burra, N. (1995), "Child Bonded Labourers in India", Judith Ennew (ed.), *op. cit.*, p. 71.

Burra, N. (1986), "Child labour in India: Poverty, Exploitation and Vested Interest", *Social Action*, 36, pp. 248-50.

Carnoy, M. (1995), "Structural adjustment and the changing face of education", *International Labour Review*, vol. 134: 6, pp. 653-73.

Centre of Concern for Child Labour (1992), *A Summary of Child Labour Report*, New Delhi, CCCL, p.4.

Challis, J. & D. Elliman (1979), *op. cit.*, pp. 17.

Challis, J. & D., Elliman (1979), *op. cit.*, p. 91.

Challis, J. & D Elliman (1979), *Child Workers Today*, Middlesex, Quartermaine House Ltd., pp. 55-6.

Challis, J. & D. Elliman (1979), *Child Workers Today*, Middlesex (U.K.), Quarter-maine House Ltd., *Chapter VII : Africa & the Middle East*, p. 91.

Challis, J. & D. Elliman (1979), *op. cit.*, p. 91.

Challis, J. & D. Elliman (1979), *op.cit.*, p. 18.

Challis, J. & D. Elliman (1979), *op.cit.*, p. 97.

Challis, J. and D. Elliman (1979), *Child Workers Today*, Middlesex, Quartermaine House Ltd.

Charoenwal, M.(1987), "Country Paper: Thailand", in PIACT (ed.), *Asian Regional Tripartite Workshop on Practical Measures to Combat Child Labour*: Proceedings & Working papers, Geneva, ILO, 271.

"Children Used to Spray Cyanide in Benguet", *Manila Chronicle*, July 27, 1992.

Children's Rights International (1990), *Children Without Childhood: Violations of Children's Right in Guatemala*, Guatemala City, C.R.I., pp. 21-22.

Clason, E. (*n.d.*), *Save the Children and Children's Rights: In a Historical Perspective*, Geneva, 15CA, pp. 17-19.

Conditions of Work Digest, vol X, 1/1991, Part II, Annex III.

CWIN (n.d.), "Carpet Factory : A Source of Foreign Currency and the Misery of Our Children", Kathmandu, CWIN, (brochure).

Dawson, G.D. (1964), "Education in Somalia", *Comparative Education Review*, No. 8., p. 201.

De Bernis, G.D. (1986), "Basic Needs and Dynamics of Development", in JASPA (ed.), *The Challenge of Employment & Basic Needs in Africa*, Nairobi, OUP, p. 30.

Deptt. of Labour (1994), *op.cit.*, p. 59, ff. no. 6.

Dimenstein, G. (1994), "Little Girls of the Night", in *Disposable Children : The Hazards of Growing up Poor in Latin America*, vol. XXVII : 6, New York, North American Congress on Latin America, pp. 29-33.

Dingwaney, M. *et.al* (1988), *Children of Drakness: A Manual on Child Labour in India*, New Delhi, Rural Labour Cell.

Dingwaney, M.et. al (1988), *Children of Darkness : A Manual on Child Labour in India*, New Delhi, N.L.I., p. 8.

Directorate of Labour Welfare & IPEC (1996), *Child Labour in the Football Manufacturing Industry*, Geneva, ILO, p. iv.

Dube, L. (1981) "The Economic Roles of Children in India: Methodological Issues", G. Rodgers & G. Standing (eds.), *op. cit*, p. 198.

Ennew, J. & B. Milne (1989), *The Next Generation: Lives of Third World Children*, London, Zed Books Ltd., pp. 173-74.

Ennew, J. and B. Milne (1989), *The Next Generation : Lives of Third World*

Countries, London, Zed Books, Table 6, p. 74 (computed from table).

Ennew, J. & B. Milne (1989), *The Next Generation: Lives of Third World Children*, London, Zed Books Ltd., pp. 16-80 (for detailed discussion).

Federation of Kenya Employers (1994), *Report on a Survey on Child Labour in Commercial Agricultural Plantations in Kenya*, Nairobi, Federation of Kenya Employers, p. 8.

Fergany, N. (1993), *Child Labour in the Arab Countries*, The Arab Council for Childhood and Development, as quoted in U.S. Deptt. of Labour, *By the Sweat & Toil of Children*, Washington D.C., July 15, 1994, pp. 62-3.

Fergany, N. (1993), *Child Labour in the Arab Countries*, the Arab Council for Childhood and Development, p. 14.

Fyfe, A (1989), *Child Labour*, Oxford, Polity Press, esp. pp. 3-5.

Fyfe, A (1989), *ChildLlabour*, Oxford, Polity Press, p. 75.

Fyfe, A (1989), *op. cit.*, p. 76.

Fyfe, A (1995), "Child Labour" in Judith Ennew (ed.), *Learning or Labouring*? Florence, International Child Development Centre, UNICEF, p. 13

Fyfe, A. (1989), *op. cit.*, pp. 15-16.

Fyfe, A. (1994), *Child Labour Policy and the Role of Education in India*, Geneva, ILO (*mimeo*), p. 2 as cited in U.S. Deptt. of Labour, *By the Sweat & Toil of Children*, Bureau of International Labour Affairs, 1994, p. 73

Fyfe, A. (1995), *op. cit.*

Gangrade, KD. & A. J. Gathia (1983), *Women and Child Workers in the Unorganised Sector*, New Delhi, Concept House Publishing Co.

Glauser, B. (1990), "Street Children: Deconstructing a construct" in James, H. & A. Prout (eds.), *Constructing and Reconstructing Childhood : Contemporary Issues in Sociological Study of Childhood*, Brighton, The Falmer Press, p. 139.

Glauser, B. (1990), *op.cit.*, pp. 139-42.

Goonesekere, S.W.E. (1993), *Child Labour in Sri Lanka*, Geneva, ILO, pp. 9-10.

Goonesekere, S.W.E. (1993), *Child Labour in Sri Lanka; Learning from the Past*, Geneva, ILO, p. 11.

Govt. of India (1981), Census of India 1981, Govt. of India, Vol. 22, Part IV-A : 13.

Guerro, E. (1993), "Children Victims and Result of Poverty in Philippines", Associated Press, June 30.

Guessous, S.N. (1994) , *The Use of Child Labour in Morocco in the Produc-*

tion of Goods Exported to the United States, Casablanca, cited in the U.S. Deptt. of Labour, *op.cit.*

Gupta, M. & K.Voll. (1987), *Young Hands at Work,* New Delhi, Atma Rama & Sons, p. 49.

Hafeez, S. (1979), *Child Labour in Pakistan,* Geneva, ILO (mimeo).

Hart, K (1973), "Informal Income Opportunities and Urban Employment in Ghana", *Journal of Modern African Studies,* March issue.

Hodgson, D. (n.d.), "Sex Tourism and Child Prostitution in Asia : Legal Responses and Strategies", Deptt. of Law, The University of Western Australia, p. 3

Human Rights Commission of Pakistan (1994), *State of Human Rights in Pakistan,* Lahore, HRCP, pp. 121-22.

ICFTU- APRO (1992), *op.cit.*

ICFTU / APRO (1993), "Country Reports in a nutshell", in sub-Regional Seminars on Child Labour, Oct., Chart 1, as cited in U.S. Deptt. of Labour, *op.cit.,* p. 27.

ICFTU-APRO (1992), *Pilot Study of Child Labour in Sivakasi,* New Delhi, ICFTU-APRO, South Asia Office, p. 4.

ICLSIT (1995), *Child Labour in India : A Perspective,* New Delhi, Govt. of India, p. 17-18.

ILO (1919), *The Minimum Age (Industry) Convention,* Geneva, ILO.

ILO (1920), *The Minimum Age (Sea) Convention,* Geneva, ILO.

ILO (1921), *The Minimum Age (Agriculture) Convention,* Geneva, ILO.

ILO (1921), *The Minimum Age (Trimmers & Stokers) Convention,* Geneva, ILO.

ILO (1930), *Convention Concerning Forced or Compulsory Labour,* C 29, Geneva, Article 2.

ILO (1930), *Convention Concerning Forced or Compulsory Labour,* Geneva, ILO, Article 2(1).

ILO (1932), *The Minimum Age (Non-Industrial Employment) Convention,* Geneva, ILO.

ILO (1936), *The Minimum Age (Sea) Convention (Revised),* Geneva, ILO.

ILO (1937), *The Minimum Age (Industry) Convention (Revised),* Geneva, ILO.

ILO (1937), *The Minimum Age (Non-Industrial Employment) Convention (Revised),* Geneva, ILO.

ILO (1959), *The Minimum Age (Fishermen) Convention,* Geneva, ILO.

ILO (1965), *The Minimum Age (Underground Work) Convention,* Geneva, ILO.

ILO (1972), *Employment, Incomes and Equity: A Strategy for Increasing Productive Employment in Keyna,* Geneva, ILO.

ILO (1973), *Minimum Age for Admission to Employment,* ILO, Article 2

Sec 3 of C 138, Minimum Age Convention, 1973.
ILO (1973), *op. cit.*
ILO (1973), *Recommendation Concerning Minimum Age for Admission to Employment*, Geneva, esp. section-II on Minimum Age of section-IV, On Conditions of Employment.
ILO (1981), *Minimum Age*, Geneva, ILO, pp. 179-209 (*List of Legislation by Country*).
ILO (1988), *Committee of Experts Report*, Geneva, ILO, p. 53.
ILO (1991), "Child Labour: Law and Practice", in *Conditions of Work Digest*, Geneva, ILO, Vol. 1, p.3.
ILO (1992), "From Work to Exploitation" in Ennew, J. (ed.), *Learning or Labouring?*, Florence, ICDC (UNICEF), 1995, p. 14.
ILO (1992), *Child Labour in Tanzania*, Geneva, ILO, p. 8.
ILO (1992), "From Work to Exploitation", *World Labour Report*, Geneva, ILO, p. 14.
ILO (1992), *Child Labour in Tanzania*, Geneva, ILO, pp. 16-17.
ILO (1992), *Children in Bondage*, Geneva, ILO.
ILO (1992), *Towards Action Against Child Labour in Zimbabwe*, Geneva, ILO, pp. 46-47.
ILO (1992), *Towards Action Against Child Labour in Zimbabwe*, Geneva, ILO.
ILO (1992), *Towards Action Against Child Labour in Zimbabwe*, Geneva, ILO, pp. 53-54.
ILO (1992), *Towards Action Against Child Labour in Zimbabwe*, Geneva, ILO.
ILO (1993), "Forced Labour" in *World Labour Report*, 1993, Geneva, ILO, p.11.
ILO (1993), *Child Labour in Indonesia*, Geneva, ILO, p. 6.
ILO (1993), *Child Labour in Indonesia*, Geneva, ILO.
ILO (1993), *Child Labour in Indonesia*, Geneva, ILO.
ILO (1993), *op.cit.*
ILO (1994), *General Report and Observations Concerning Particular Countries*, Geneva, ILO, p. 135.
ILO (1994), *Report of the Committee of Experts on the Application of Conventions and Recommendations : General Report and Observations Concerning Particular Countries*, Geneva, ILO, p. 135.
ILO (1994), *Report of the Committee of Experts on the Application of Conventions and Recommendations*, Geneva, ILO, Report III, part 4a, pp. 61-62.
ILO (1995), *International Child Labour Hearing*, U.S. Department of Labour, quoted in *By the Sweat & Toil of Children*, Vol. II, U.S. Deptt. of Labour, p. 21.

ILO (1995), *In the Twilight Zone : Child Workers in the Hotel, Tourism and Catering Industry*, Geneva, ILO, pp. 8, 20-21.

ILO (1996), "A Framework for Trade Union Policy and Action to Combat Child Labour", *Labour Education*, Vol. 1, No. 102, p.12

ILO (1996), *Trade Unions and Child Labour*, 102, Geneva, ILO, pp.3-4.

ILO (1998), *Child Labour*, Geneva, ILO, Report VI (2), Question, 4, p.28.

ILO (1998), *Child Labour: The ILO in Asia and the Pacific*, Bangkok, the ILO Regional Office, p.5.

ILO (1998), *op.cit.*, pp. 16-19.

ILO (1999), *Child Labour, Report IV, 2 B*, Geneva, ILO.

ILO (1999), *Child Labour, Report IV, 2 B*, Geneva, ILO, pp. 11-13.

ILO (1999), *Child Labour, Report IV, 2 B*, Geneva, ILO, p. 13.

JASPA (1986), "The Informal Sector in Africa", in JASPA (ed.), *The Challenge of Employment & Basic Needs in Africa*, Nairobi, Oxford University Press, p. 259.

JASPA (1986), "The informal Sector in Africa", in JASPA/ILO (ed), *op.cit.*, pp. 244-60.

JASPA (1986), *op.cit.*, p. 247.

JASPA (1986), *The Challenge of Employment & Basic Needs in Africa*, Nairobi, Oxford University Press, pp. 249-53.

Jome, K.S. et. al (1993), *Child Workers in Asia*, vol. 9 : 2, Apr- June, pp. 18-19

Kane, A. Salan (1995), "The Work of Child Nomads", in J. Ennew (ed.), *op. cit.*, p. 68.

Kane, A.S. (1995), "The Work of Child Nomads" , in J. Ennew (ed.), *Learning or Labouring?*, Florence, ICDC (UNICEF), p. 68.

Kearney, N. (1996) "There is not a Moment to Lose...", *ibid*, p. 8.

Kponhassia, G. (1993), Child Labour in the Mines of Cote d' Ivoire (in French) New York, UNICEF/DCI, pp. 6-8, cited in the U.S. Deptt. of Labour, *op.cit*, p. 58-59.

Kulkarni, M.N. "*Match-making children in Sivakasi*", *Economic and Political Weekly*, XVIII, 43, pp. 185-6.

Lavers, A. (1960), "Schooling in Massailand", *Kenya Education Journal*, No. 1

Leeten, G.K. (2001), "Child Labour, Questions on Magnitude", in Leeten and White, *Child Labour, Policy Perspective*, Aksant Academic Publishers, Amsterdan, pp. 47-66.

Lee-Wright, P. (1990), *Child Slaves*, London, Earthscan.

Loewenson, R. (1995), *Child labour in Commercial Agriculture in Zimbabwe: Report of a Case Study*, Harare, IPECL (ILO) p. 8.

Macaranas, J. (1994), *Child Labour in The Philippines*, Washington D.C., ILRERF, pp. 5-6.

Mahajan, K. & J. Gathia (1992), *Child Labour : An Analytical Study*, New Delhi, CCCL, p. 27.

Mahmood, Z. et. al. (1991), *Child Labour in Brick-Kiln Industries*, Lahore University of Punjab.

Maier, H. (1996), "Even the poorest people recognize...", *Labour Education, op.cit.*, pp. 2-3.

Maldonado, Carlos (1995), "The Informal Sector: Legalization or Laissez-faire," *International Labour Review*, Vol. 134: 6, p 173.

Marla, S. (1977) "Bonded Labour in Medak District, *A.P.*" *NLI Bulletin*, 3: 10, pp. 424 & 430.

Ministry of Labour & Human Welfare (1999), *Situation Analysis of Street Children in Eritrea: National Survey Report*, Asmara (Eritrea), MLHW, p. 4.

Morice, A (1981), "The Exploitation of Children in the 'Informal Sector': Proposals for Research", in Gerry Rodgers and Guy Standing (eds.), *Child Work, Poverty and Underdevelopment*, Geneva, ILO, p. 150.

Morice, A (1981), "The Exploitation of Children in the 'Informal Sector': Proposals for Research", in G. Rodgers & G. Standing (eds.), *Child Work, Poverty and Underdevelopment*, Geneva, ILO, p. 137.

Morice, A (1981), *op. cit.*, p. 136.

Morice, A (1981), *op. cit.*, p. 136.

Morice, A (1981), *op. cit.*, p. 144.

Morice, A (1981), *op.cit.*, p. 145.

Morice, A. (1981), *"The Exploitation of children in the 'Informal Sector' : Proposals for Research"*, in G. Rodgers & G. Standing (eds.), *Child Work, Poverty and Underdevelopment*, Geneva, ILO. p. 132.

Morice, A. (1981), *op. cit.*, p. 145.

Muntarbhorn, V. (1997), A Source Book for Reporting under the Convention on the Rights of the Child, Bangkok, UNICEF, pp. 14-19.

Muntarbhorn, V. (1997), *Case Study: Thailand*, in Muntarbhorn, V., *op.cit.*, p. 56.

Nangia, P. (1991), "The situation of working children in India, in W.E. Myers (ed.), *Protecting Working Children*, London, Zed Books, 1999, p. 51.

National Youth Bureau (1996), *Thailands' Report on the Implementation of the Convention on the Rights of the Child*, Bangkok, Prime Minister's Office & NYB, p. 131.

NCRC/UNICEF (1993), *Children and Women in South Africa: A Situation Analysis*, Johannesburg, UNICEF.

News from Brazil, No. 172, Mar. 30, 1995.

NGO Coalition for Monitoring the CRC (1994), *Supplementary Report*,

Manila, *NGO Coalition for Monitoring the Convention on the Rights of the Child*, pp. 18.

Onyongo, Philista P.M. (1988), *op.cit.*

Onyongo, Philista, P.M. (1988), "Child Labour Policies and Programmes in Kenya", in Bequele, A & Jo Boydem (eds.), *Combating Child Labour,* Geneva, ILO, p. 162.

Operations Research Group (1993), *Child Labour in Different Industries: Consolidated Report*, Madras (Chennai).

Pereira, I. & R.L.B. Rosa (1993), *Child Labour in the Footwear Industry in Franca*, Geneva, ILO.

Phadke, S (1995), "Eleven-year Old Girls Gets Deliverance From Sea of Bonded Labour", *Bombay Times*, Feb. 14.

Pinlac, Amparo B. (1987), "Country Paper: Philippines", in PIACT (ed.) *op.cit.*, p. 308.

Pradhan, G. (1993), *Misery Behind the Looms; Child Labourers in the Carpet Factories in Nepal*, Kathmandu, CWIN, pp. 19, 26.

Querenghi, G. (1996), "A New Trade Union Onslaught Against Child Labour, in Trade Unions and Child Labour", *Labour Education*, Vol.1, No. 102, p.1.

Raasta (1996), An Assessment of the Working Child in the Soccer Ball Industry, Lahore, Raasta Development Consultants, p. 19.

Rahman, H. (1992), *Situation of Child Domestic Services*, Dhaka, UNICEF, p. 12.

Rosario, del R. (1990), Sub contracting Networks in the Garment Industry in Taytay and Angono, Rizal, Manila, The Philippines University / UNICEF, p. 11.

Reimers, F. & L. Tiburcio, (1993), *Education, Adjustment and Reconstruction Options for Change*, Paris, UNESCO, p. 14.

Rialp, V. (1993), *Children and hazardous work in the Philippines*, Geneva, ILO.

Ritcher, K. & Ard-am, O (1995), *Child Labour in Thailand's Fishing Industry*, Salaya, Nakhon Pathom, Mahidol University, Table 1,4 also pp. 16-21.

Rodgers, G. & G. Standing (1981), "The Economic Roles of Children : Issues for Analysis", in G. Rodgers & G. Standing (eds.), *op. cit.*, p. 13.

Rodgers, G. & G. Standing (1981), "The Economic Roles of Children : Issues for Analysis", in Gerry Rodgers & Guy Standing (eds.), *op. cit.*, pp. 2-11.

Rodgers, G. & G. Standing (1981), *op. cit.*, pp. 1-45, esp. Section II.

Rosario, A. (1988), "Ragpicking and Ragpickers' education and Development Scheme in Bangalore City", *Country Reports & Case*

Studies presented at the Second Regional Conference on Child Abuse and Neglect, Feb. 8-13, Bangkok, (Thailand).

Rosenzweing, M.R. (1981), "Household and Non-household Activities of Youth: Issues of Modeling, Data and Estimation Strategies", in G. Rodgers & G. Standing (eds.), *op. cit.*, p. 233.

Sattaur, O. (1993), *Child Labour in Nepal*, Kathmandu, Child Workers in Nepal Concerned Center.

Sawyer, R. (1988), *Children Enslaved*, London, Routledge, p. 47.

Schibotto, G. & A. Cussianovich (1994), *Working Children; Building an Identity*, Lima Peru, Manthoc, p. 66.

Schibotto, G. & A. Cussianovich (1994), *Working Children: Building an Identity*, Lima Peru, Manthoc, p. 31.

Schibotto, G. & A. Cussianovich, *op.cit.*, p. 66.

Schibotto, G.& A. Cussianovich (1994), *Working Children : Building an Identity*, Lima, Manthoc, p. 27.

Schildkrout, E. (1981), "The Employment of Children in Kano (Nigeria)", in Gerry Rodgers & Guy Standing (eds.), *op. cit.*, pp. 81-112.

Schildkrout, E. (1981), "The Employment of Children in Kano (Nigeria)" in G. Rodgers & G. Standing (eds.), *Child Work, Poverty and Underdevelopment*, Geneva, ILO, p. 99.

Schildkrout, E. (1981), *op. cit.*, pp. 81-106, exp. pp. 99-105.

see Country Reports on Human Rights Practices, U.S. Deptt. of State, Feb. 1995.

Shepherd, A.W. (1979), "The Development of Capitalist Rice Farming in Northern Ghana", Combridge, Ph.D. Dissertation.

Slazar, Maria Cristina *et. al* (1994), Child Labour in Industrial Sectors in Colombia, Santafe de Bogota, cited in U.S. Deptt. of Labour (1994), *op.cit.*, pp. 50-51.

Sutton, A. (1994), *Slavery in Brazil*, London, Anti-Slavery International, p. 84.

Sutton, A. (1994), *Slavery in Brazil*, London, Anti-Slavery International, p. 93.

Torry, W. (1973), *Subsistence Ecology among the Gabra: Nomads of the Kenya, Ethopia Frontier, Ph.D. Dissertaion*, Columbia University, (mimeo), pp. 156-62.

U.N. (1956), *Supplementary Convention on the Abolition of Slavery, the Slave Trade and Institutions and Practices Similar to Slavery*, Sept. 7, and enforced on April 30, 1957, 266 UNTS 3.

U.N. (1975), *Poverty, Unemployment and Development Policy: A case study of selected issues with reference to Kerala*, New York, U.N. esp. pp. 121-26.

U.N. (1997), *Doc. A/49/478*, Oct, 5, p. 29.

U.N. *Document E/CN.4/sub.2/199/NGO/15*, p. 3.

U.N.(1989), *Convention on the Rights of the Child*, Article 32, sections (1) & (2) especially sub-section 2(a).

U.S. Deptt. of Labour (1994), *op.cit.*, p. 109.

U.S. Deptt. of Labour (1994), *op.cit.*, p. 126 ff No. 2.

U.S. Deptt. of Labour (1975), *op. cit.*, p. 29.

U.S. Deptt. of Labour (1994), *By the Sweat & Toil of Children*, Washington D.C., p. 74.

U.S. Deptt. of labour (1994), *By the Sweat & Toil of Children*, Washington D.C., Bureau of International Labour Affairs, p. 6.

U.S. Deptt. of Labour (1994), *op. cit.* cited Bonded Labour Liberation Front, Mirzapur, ff 28, p. 77.

U.S. Deptt. of Labour (1994), *op. cit.*, pp. 115-16.

U.S. Deptt. of Labour (1994), *op.cit.*, citing letter from UMT to International Child Labour Study (June 22), p. 114.

U.S. Deptt. of Labour (1994), *op.cit.*, p. 130.

U.S. Deptt. of Labour (1994), *op.cit.*, p. 139, referring to the ILO Study of 1988 .

U.S. Deptt. of Labour (1994), *op.cit.*, p. 164.

U.S. Deptt. of Labour (1994), *op.cit.*, p. 27.

U.S. Deptt. of Labour (1994), *op.cit.*, p. 28 ff.

U.S. Deptt. of Labour (1994), *op.cit.*, p. 36.

U.S. Deptt. of Labour (1994), *op.cit.*, p. 60 .

U.S. Deptt. of Labour (1994), *op.cit.*, p. 81.

U.S. Deptt. of Labour (1994), *op.cit.*, p. 83.

U.S. Deptt. of Labour (1995), *By the Sweat & Toil of Children*, Vol II. The Use of Child labour in U.S. Agricultural Imports & Forced and Bonded Child Labour, Washington D.C., Bureau of International Labour Affairs, esp. pp. 77-149.

U.S. Deptt. of Labour (1995), *By the Sweat & Toil of Children*, Vol II, Washington D.C. Bureau of International Labour Affairs, p. 41.

U.S. Deptt. of State (1994), *Country Reports on Human Rights Practices for 1993*, Washington D.C., U.S. Deptt. of State, p. 502.

U.S.Deptt. of Labour (1995), *By the Sweat & Toil of Children*, Vol II, Washington, D.C., Bureau of International Labour Affairs, pp. 25-30.

UN (1993), *Doc. CRC/C/3/Add. 23*, p. 54.

UN Commission on Human Rights (1994), *U.N. Doc. E/CN.4/1994/84*, p.20.

UNDP (1992), *World Report on Human Development*, Paris, Economica.

UNICEF (1989), "Thai Children At Work", in *The Situation Analysis for Women and Children*, New York, UNICEF, p. 27.

UNICEF (1991), *The Situation of Women and Children in Lesotho*, Maseru, Ministry of Planning, Economic and Manpower, in collaboration with UNICEF, p. 127.

UNICEF (1992), *Child Labour in the Carpet Weaving Industry in Punjab*, Punjab (Pakistan), UNICEF, p. 7.

UNICEF (1992), *Situation Analysis of Children and Women in Pakistan*, Islamabad, UNICEF, p. 83.

UNICEF (1993), *Situation Analysis on Women and Children in Indonesia*, New York, UNICEF, p. 252.

UNICEF (2000), *The State of the World's Children 2000*, New York/ Geneva, UNICEF, p.24.

UNICEF, MOJ (1989), Child Labour Legislation in Egypt, Cairo, UNICEF & Egyptian Ministry of Justice, pp. 126-29.

Van Hear, N. (1982), "Child Labour and the Development of Capitalist Agriculture in Ghana", *Development and Change*, 13:4, pp. 499-514.

Van Hear, N. (1995), "Child Labour and the Development of Capitalist Agriculture in Ghana", in Judith Ennew (ed.), *op. cit.*, p. 62.

Van Hear, N. (1995), "Child Labour and the Development of Capitalist Agriculture in Ghana", in Judith Ennew (ed.), *Learning or Labouring?*, Florence, UNICEF, p. 62.

Van Oosterhout (1988), "Child Labour in the Philippines: The Muro-amdeep- sea fishing operation' in ILO (ed.), *Combating Child Labour, op cit.* p. 111.

Vijaygopalan, S. (1993), *Child Labour in the Carpet Industry: A Status Report*, New Delhi, NCAER, pp. 43-44.

Weiner, M. (1991), *The Child and the State in India*, Princeton, OUP, pp. 191-96.

White, B.& I. Tjandraningsih (n.d.), *Rural Children in the Industrialization Process: Child and Youth Labour in 'Traditional' and 'Modern' Industries in West Java*, (mss), pp. 19-20 as cited in U.S. Deptt. of Labour (1994), *op.cit.*, p. 96.

William Malya (1995), National Programme Co-ordinator, International Programme for the Elimination of Child labour, Dar-ES-Salaam, June 20, in an interview by Deptt. of Labour Official, cited in U.S. Deptt. of labour, *op.cit*, p. 36.